Experiencing the Miracles of Jesus

KAY ARTHUR
PETE De LACY

HARVEST HOUSE PUBLISHERS

EUGENE, OREGON

Cover by Koechel Peterson & Associates, Minneapolis, Minnesota

EXPERIENCING THE MIRACLES OF JESUS
Copyright © 2010 by Precept Ministries International
Published by Harvest House Publishers
Eugene, Oregon 97402
www.harvesthousepublishers.com

Library of Congress Cataloging-in-Publication Data
Arthur, Kay
Experiencing the miracles of Jesus / Kay Arthur and Pete De Lacy.
    p. cm.—(The new inductive study series)
Includes bibliographical references.
ISBN 978-0-7369-2513-6 (pbk.)
1. Bible. N.T. Mark—Textbooks. 2. Jesus Christ—Miracles—Textbooks. I. De Lacy, Pete. II. Title.
BS2586A78 2010
.226.30071—dc22
                                                                    2009016294

Printed in the United States of America

10 11 12 13 14 15 16 17 / BP-SK / 10 9 8 7 6 5 4 3 2 1

CONTENTS

∾∾∾∾∾

How to Get Started...

Reading directions is sometimes difficult and hardly ever enjoyable! Most often you just want to get started. Only if all else fails will you read the instructions. We understand, but please don't approach this study that way. These brief instructions are a vital part of getting started on the right foot! These few pages will help you immensely.

FIRST

As you study Mark, you will need four things in addition to this book:

1. A Bible that you are willing to mark in. The marking is essential. An ideal Bible for this purpose is *The New Inductive Study Bible (NISB)*. The *NISB* is in a single-column text format with large, easy-to-read type, which is ideal for marking. The margins of the text are wide and blank so you can take notes.

The *NISB* also has instructions for studying each book of the Bible, but it does not contain any commentary on the text, nor is it compiled from any theological stance. Its purpose is to teach you how to discern truth for yourself through the inductive method of study. (The various charts and maps that you will find in the appendix of this study guide are taken from the *NISB*.)

Whichever Bible you use, just know you will need to mark in it, which brings us to the second item you will need...

2. A fine-point, four-color ballpoint pen or various colored fine-point pens you can use to write in your Bible. Office supply stores should have these.

3. Colored pencils or an eight-color leaded Pentel pencil.

4. A composition book or a notebook for working on your assignments and recording your insights.

SECOND

1. As you study Mark, you will be given specific instructions for each day's study. These should take you between 20 and 30 minutes a day, but if you spend more time than this, you will increase your intimacy with the Word of God and the God of the Word.

If you are doing this study in a class and you find the lessons too heavy, simply do what you can. To do a little is better than to do nothing. Don't be an all-or-nothing person when it comes to Bible study.

Remember, anytime you get into the Word of God, you enter into more intensive warfare with the devil (our enemy). Why? Every piece of the Christian's armor is related to the Word of God. And our one and only offensive weapon is the sword of the Spirit, which is the Word of God. The enemy wants you to have a dull sword. Don't cooperate! You don't have to!

2. As you read each chapter, train yourself to ask the "5 W's and an H": who, what, when, where, why, and how. Asking questions like these helps you see exactly what the Word of God is saying. When you interrogate the text with the 5 W's and an H, you ask questions like these:

What is the chapter about?

Who are the main characters?

When does this event or teaching take place?

Where does this happen?

Why is this being done or said?

How did it happen?

3. Locations are important in many books of the Bible, so marking references to these in a distinguishable way will be helpful to you. We simply underline every reference to a location in green (grass and trees are green!) using a four-color ballpoint pen. Maps are included in the appendix of this study so you can look up the locations.

4. References to time are also very important and should be marked in an easily recognizable way in your Bible. We mark them by putting a clock like this 🕐 in the margin of the Bible beside the verse where the phrase occurs. You may want to underline or color the references to time in one specific color.

5. You will be given certain key words to mark throughout this study. This is the purpose of the colored pencils and the colored pens. If you will develop the habit of marking your Bible in this way, you will find it will make a significant difference in the effectiveness of your study and in how much you remember.

A key word is an important word that the author uses repeatedly in order to convey his message to his readers. Certain key words will show up throughout Mark; others will be concentrated in specific chapters. When you mark a key word, you should also mark its synonyms (words that mean the same thing in the context) and any pronouns (*I, me, my, mine; you, your, yours; he, him, his; she, her, hers;*

it, *its*; *we, us, our, ours*; *they, them, their, theirs*) in the same way you have marked the key word. Also, mark each word the same way in all of its forms (such as *judge, judgment*, and *judging*).We will give you a few suggestions for ways to mark key words in your daily assignments.

You can use colors or symbols or a combination of colors and symbols to mark words for easy identification. However, colors are easier to distinguish than symbols. When we use symbols, we keep them very simple. For example, you could draw a red heart around the word *love* and shade the inside of the heart like this: love.

When we mark the members of the Godhead (which we do not always mark), we color each word yellow and mark *Father* with a purple triangle like this: **Father.** We mark *Son* this way: **Son** and *Holy Spirit* this way: **Spirit.**

Mark key words in a way that is easy for you to remember.

Devising a color-coding system for marking key words throughout your Bible will help you instantly see where a key word is used. To keep track of your key words, list them on a three-by-five card and mark them the way you mark them in your Bible. You can use this card as a bookmark.

6. A chart called MARK AT A GLANCE is included at the back of this book. As you complete your study of a chapter, record the main theme of that chapter under the appropriate chapter number. The main theme of a chapter is what the chapter deals with the most. It may be a particular subject or teaching.

If you fill out the MARK AT A GLANCE chart as you progress through the study, you will have a synopsis of Mark when you are finished. If you have a copy of *The New Inductive Study Bible,* you will find the same chart on page 1650. If you record your themes there, you will have them for a ready reference.

7. Always begin your study with prayer. As you do your part to handle the Word of God accurately, you must remember that the Bible is a divinely inspired book. The words that you are reading are truth, given to you by God so you can know Him and His ways more intimately. These truths are divinely revealed.

> For to us God revealed them through the Spirit; for the Spirit searches all things, even the depths of God. For who among men knows the thoughts of a man except the spirit of the man which is in him? Even so the thoughts of God no one knows except the Spirit of God (1 Corinthians 2:10-11).

Therefore ask God to reveal His truth to you as He leads and guides you into all truth. He will if you will ask.

8. Each day when you finish your lesson, meditate on what you saw. Ask your heavenly Father how you should live in light of the truths you have just studied. At times, depending on how God has spoken to you through His Word, you might even want to write LFL ("Lessons for Life") in the margin of your Bible and then, as briefly as possible, record the lesson for life that you want to remember.

THIRD

This study is set up so that you have an assignment for every day of the week—so that you are in the Word daily. If you work through your study in this way, you will benefit more than if you do a week's study in one sitting. Pacing yourself this way allows time for thinking through what you learn on a daily basis!

The seventh day of each week differs from the other six days. The seventh day is designed to aid group discussion;

however, it's also profitable if you are studying this book individually.

The "seventh" day is whatever day in the week you choose to finish your week's study. On this day, you will find a verse or two for you to memorize and Store in Your Heart. Then there is a passage to Read and Discuss. This will help you focus on a major truth or major truths covered in your study that week.

We have included Questions for Discussion or Individual Study to assist those using this book in a Sunday school class or a group Bible study. Taking the time to answer these questions will help you apply the truth to your own life even if you are not doing this study with anyone else.

If you are in a group, be sure every member of the class, including the teacher, supports his or her answers and insights from the Bible text itself. Then you will be handling the Word of God accurately. As you learn to see what the text says and compare Scripture with Scripture, the Bible explains itself.

Always examine your insights by carefully observing the text to see what it *says*. Then, before you decide what the passage of Scripture *means*, make sure that you interpret it in the light of its context. Scripture will never contradict Scripture. If it ever seems to contradict the rest of the Word of God, you can be certain that something is being taken out of context. If you come to a passage that is difficult to understand, reserve your interpretations for a time when you can study the passage in greater depth.

The purpose of the Thought for the Week is to share with you what we consider to be an important element in your week of study. We have included it for your evaluation and, we hope, for your edification. This section will help you see how to walk in light of what you learned.

Books in the New Inductive Study Series are survey courses. If you want to do a more in-depth study of a particular book of the Bible, we suggest you do a Precept Upon Precept Bible study course on that book. You may obtain more information on these courses by contacting Precept Ministries International at 800-763-8280, visiting our website at www.precept.org, or filling out and mailing the response card in the back of this book.

INTRODUCTION TO MARK

The first four books of the New Testament are called the Gospels. The English word *gospel* is the translation of the Greek word *euaggelion*, which means "good news." These four books give us different pictures of Jesus Christ, the main subject of the good news. They're all about Him—who He is and what He has done for us. The Gospel of Mark is Mark's account of this good news.

The first three Gospels—Matthew, Mark, and Luke—are frequently referred to as the *synoptic* Gospels, meaning they are written with the same eye or from the same point of view. By comparing and contrasting their somewhat parallel accounts, you can notice their unique perspectives and emphases.

Matthew begins with a genealogy, showing that Jesus is the promised descendant of Abraham and David, the deliverer whom the Old Testament prophecies predicted would come. In fact, Matthew quotes many Old Testament messianic prophecies throughout his Gospel, so he was probably writing primarily to a Jewish audience. Mark wrote from his own perspective and with his own purpose, so his account differs from Matthew's. The same is true for Luke's Gospel.

Mark's style is also unique. You'll see that he gets right to the point quickly, with little amplification. Because of that, Mark is the shortest of the Gospels.

As we are studying the Gospels, we don't need to cross-reference every teaching and event to build a "harmony" of the Gospels—a number of authors have done this work for us. In fact, you'll find a concise harmony of the Gospels in *The New Inductive Study Bible* on pages 2117–2122. Such charts show at a glance where a particular teaching or event occurs in the other Gospels or whether it is included in just one. Such a harmony may be helpful at times, but we're going to stick to studying Mark's Gospel, only occasionally referring to the others for specific points that are so delicious and nutritious, we don't want you to miss the treat!

Most scholars believe that the author of Mark is John Mark of Acts 12. There we learn that after Peter was released by an angel from the jail Herod had imprisoned him in, he went to the house of Mary the mother of John, where many of the brethren were praying. This John was also called Mark.

When Barnabas and Saul returned to Antioch from Jerusalem, they took Mark with them. He started out with Paul and Barnabas on their first missionary journey, but then he left them and returned to Jerusalem. For this, Paul refused to take Mark with him on his second missionary journey, but Barnabas (Mark's cousin, according to Colossians 4:10) left with Mark separately. By the end of Paul's ministry, he had evidently reconciled with Mark (2 Timothy 4:11).

Tradition says that Mark served with Peter and that Peter told Mark all he had seen and heard during his time with Jesus. Mark's short, sharp, direct, quick-to-the-point style does sound something like the impetuous Peter the Gospels and Acts describe. Matthew and John were two of Jesus' 12 disciples, but Mark and Luke were not—they heard firsthand accounts but were not eyewitnesses. But like all the authors of the books of the Bible, they wrote under the inspiration of the Holy Spirit, so their recorded accounts are true—just as much God's Word as any other book of the Bible.

As we study Mark together, we'll focus on the message, not the messenger; we'll "fix our eyes on Jesus, the author and perfecter of our faith" (Hebrews 12:2).

MARK

THE SON OF GOD

∾∾∾∾

When John baptized Jesus, Jesus "saw the heavens opening, and the Spirit like a dove descending upon Him; and a voice came out of the heavens: 'You are My beloved Son, in You I am well-pleased'" (Mark 1:10-11). The Father recognized Jesus and proclaimed Him to be His Son, but now the question is, who else will acknowledge Him? Will the Jews, or will anyone else? How about you—are you prepared to hear the truth, see with new eyes, and tell others what you learn?

DAYS ONE & TWO

As you read any book of the Bible, you'll notice that the author emphasizes subjects by repeating key words and phrases. Marking these key words with distinctive colors or symbols (or both) is an important technique that helps you carefully observe the text. You'll be marking many of these words and phrases throughout Mark, so to keep track of them, record them (and the way you plan to mark them) on a three-by-five card and use this as a bookmark throughout your study. Keeping up with key words this way as you go from chapter to chapter will help you be consistent and save time.

Read Mark 1, marking the following words and

including them on your bookmark: *God, Jesus, Holy Spirit, Satan, unclean spirits, John the Baptist, gospel,*[1] *authority, forgive(ness), believe,* and *sins.*

Be sure to double underline in green all geographical references, and mark time references with a green clock or color them green. Note the repetition of *immediately*[2] as a time reference. This is a key term throughout Mark, so you'll want to add it to your bookmark and mark it uniquely so it jumps out at you.

Be sure to ask the 5 W's and an H as you mark. This will help you focus on what the author is saying.

DAYS THREE & FOUR

Don't forget to begin your study time with prayer. Remember, you have access to the Author, who truly wants you to know, understand, and live by every word that comes from His mouth.

Today make lists of what you learn from marking the key words and time references. Keep asking the 5 W's and an H and listing the answers. Time references answer the question, when did this happen?

DAY FIVE

Read through the chapter again, and in the margin of your Bible, use a pencil to divide the major events or subjects with a horizontal line. Label each section of the chapter with the name of the most significant event or subject.

Now, who are the main characters and what is the subject of verses 1 through 11? What do you learn about God in these verses?

Read Malachi 3:1, which is quoted in Mark 1:2. Also read Isaiah 40:3, which is quoted in Mark 1:3. What do you learn about the relationship between John the Baptist and Jesus?

What did John preach? Read the following verses to gain greater insight about this topic:

> Deuteronomy 30:1-3
>
> Isaiah 55:6-9
>
> Isaiah 44:21-23
>
> Jeremiah 3:11-15

What do you learn about relationships between the Holy Spirit and Jesus and between Jesus and Satan in verses 12-13? List what happened when Jesus came up out of the water. Do you see evidence of a triune God? If so, what is the evidence?

Compare verses 14-15 with verse 4. What do you learn about Jesus' message?

To grasp what the Jews understood about the coming kingdom of God, read the following passages:

> 1 Samuel 8:6-7
>
> Psalm 47
>
> Daniel 4:24-26
>
> Daniel 7:13-14
>
> Psalm 103:19

DAY SIX

What do you learn about Jesus' teaching in the rest of the chapter? Whom does He teach? What does He teach?

How do the people respond? How does His teaching compare to the scribes' teaching? What does this tell you about Jesus?

What do you learn about Jesus' acts? How do they relate to His teaching? What is Jesus' relationship with unclean spirits (demons)?

Who recognizes Jesus as the Son of God? What does He tell them?

Determine a theme for this chapter and record it on MARK AT A GLANCE in the appendix.

DAY SEVEN

 Store in your heart: Mark 1:11
Read and discuss: Mark 1

QUESTIONS FOR DISCUSSION OR INDIVIDUAL STUDY

- Discuss the relationship between John the Baptist and Jesus. Consider the first group of Old Testament references included in day 5 and compare their messages.

- What did you learn about Jesus' teachings?

- What did you learn about the kingdom of God?

- Discuss what you learned about repentance and faith.

- Discuss Jesus' deeds and the way they relate to His teachings.

- Who were Jesus' first followers, and what were their relationships?

- What truths from Mark 1 can you apply to your life?

THOUGHT FOR THE WEEK

God sent John the Baptist to prepare the way for Jesus. John preached a baptism of repentance for the forgiveness of sins, and many people from Judea came to him for baptism, confessing their sins. He also preached about One coming after him who was mightier, One who would baptize with the Holy Spirit and not just with water.

Then one day Jesus came from Nazareth, and John baptized Him. As he did, the Holy Spirit descended on Jesus, and a voice from heaven said, "You are My beloved Son, in You I am well-pleased." Here we have God the Father, God the Son, and God the Holy Spirit all playing a part in the beginning of Jesus' earthly ministry. Just as all three Persons were present and active in the *creation* of the world, they are present and active in the *redemption* of the world.

The first man and woman God created sinned, bringing on all creation the penalty of sin and death, which continues to hold the world captive today. Paul tells us in Romans that we are groaning as we long for the redemption of our bodies. He also tells us that all creation groans as well, longing for the new heaven and earth.

God broke into human history in the person of Jesus Christ, God incarnate, the only Son of God, who for the joy set before Him voluntarily became man to identify with us and atone for our sins. Mark does not add details of Jesus' birth, but Jesus was born of a virgin so that He did not inherit a sin nature from Adam. He was perfectly obedient; He committed no sin. Everyone else that John baptized confessed their sins. But Jesus, the sinless God incarnate, had no sins to confess. He didn't need to be forgiven.

Yet Jesus subjected Himself to John's baptism of repentance, and God was pleased with Him. This event shows Jesus' identification with you and me, who *do* need to confess sins, who *do* need to repent, who *do* need to be baptized for the forgiveness of sins.

> Therefore, since the children share in flesh and blood, He Himself likewise also partook of the same, that through death He might render powerless him who had the power of death, that is, the devil, and might free those who through fear of death were subject to slavery all their lives (Hebrews 2:14-15).

The Father's testimony and the Spirit's descent (just as a dove would descend) at Jesus' baptism inaugurated Jesus' redeeming work, which culminated in His death, burial, resurrection, and ascension to the right hand of God. Following Jesus' baptism, the Spirit led Him into the wilderness for 40 days, where He was tempted by Satan. The other Gospels give details about the temptations, but Mark cuts right to the sequence—Jesus is baptized, and God is pleased; He is tempted, and angels minister to Him. Then the scene shifts right into Jesus' public ministry.

John had preached that people should repent and be baptized for the forgiveness of sins. Now Jesus announces that the time is fulfilled, the kingdom of God is at hand, and the people should repent and believe the gospel. The forerunner has done his work, preparing the way for the One who followed—the One who was mightier than John and is mightier than you, me, and even Satan. Jesus, the Son of God, has begun to call men and women to Himself, inviting them to follow Him, to believe in Him. He is ready now to reveal His power over sickness, over the spirit realm, and over the whole creation.

The people who see and hear Jesus are amazed at His authority. But they haven't seen anything yet; He's just begun!

YOUR SINS ARE FORGIVEN

When you're sick, what do you do? You go to a doctor, right? Or you may try an over-the-counter medication to save time and money. But if your sickness is sin, what medication can you try? What specialist treats this disease? Actually there is one, but you can't find Him in a doctor's office. Jesus is that Specialist; He's the Great Physician of all time! And He makes house calls! In fact, He says "I stand at the door and knock; if anyone hears My voice and opens the door, I will come in to him and will dine with him, and he with Me" (Revelation 3:20). What a precious promise that is! How many specialists do you know who can do that?

Aren't you thrilled, Beloved, that you're getting to know Him better through this wonderful Gospel of Mark?

DAY ONE

Now read Mark 2, marking the key words on your bookmark. Note the title Jesus gives Himself, mark it in a special way, and add it to your bookmark. Also mark *faith*, *Pharisees*, and *scribes*[3] and add them to your bookmark. *Pharisees* and *scribes* don't appear in every chapter, but you'll see them again.

25

Don't miss the time phrase *Sabbath* in this chapter. If you want, you can mark it in a special way. Some people like to use the number 7 because the Sabbath was the seventh day of the week.

DAY TWO

Make lists of what you learned from marking your key words. Don't let this be a rote exercise. Ask the 5 W's and an H as you go, and think about the subjects you're observing. What does Jesus say and do?

DAY THREE

Read Mark 2 again. In the margin of your Bible, note the main events that occur. Also note the questions people ask and the answers they receive.

Finally, think about what you have seen these three days, determine the main subject of this chapter, and record it on MARK AT A GLANCE in the appendix.

DAY FOUR

Read Mark 3, marking key words and phrases from your bookmark. Be sure to ask who, what, when, where, why, and how as you go. This will help you read with purpose and engage in learning instead of just coloring. And it will slow you down so you can focus on what's being taught. Don't miss *forgive(n)* in this chapter.

And watch for geographic references. Look in the

appendix at the map called "Regions from Which People Came to See Jesus" to see how far people came.

DAY FIVE

Following our pattern when we observe a chapter, make lists today from the key words and phrases you marked yesterday. Be sure to keep asking those 5 W's and an H. Everything you add to your lists is an answer to one of those questions.

DAY SIX

Read Mark 3 again and note the events as well as the teachings—the challenges and answers—in the margin of your Bible.

Note the flow from Mark 2 to Mark 3. Watch as the focus remains on a certain idea even when the location and audience change. What is the common idea?

Compare Mark 3:21 with verses 31-32. You've seen people react to Jesus in different ways, but how did His own family—at least His brothers and mother—respond to Him?

Record the theme of Mark 3 on MARK AT A GLANCE.

DAY SEVEN

Store in your heart: Mark 3:35
Read and discuss: Mark 2–3

QUESTIONS FOR DISCUSSION OR INDIVIDUAL STUDY

- ∞ Move through these two chapters event by event, covering actions, objections, questions, challenges to Jesus, and His responses.

- ∞ What did you learn in these two chapters about the forgiveness of sin?

- ∞ Who opposed Jesus? What were their objections? Do these objections occur today? Who opposes Jesus today?

- ∞ What does Jesus have authority over?

- ∞ Discuss who Jesus' brothers and sisters are according to Mark 3. What application can you make to your own life? Do you share a "family resemblance" with Jesus?

THOUGHT FOR THE WEEK

It is not those who are healthy who need a physician, but those who are sick; I did not come to call the righteous, but sinners (Mark 2:17).

All three synoptic Gospels record this statement, although it varies a bit from author to author. Luke, for example, adds that Jesus called sinners "to repentance." Matthew prefaces the comment with Hosea 6:6: "I desire compassion, and not sacrifice" (Matthew 9:13).

Why does Jesus use the metaphor of sickness when referring to His call? What's the point? We often call Jesus the Great Physician because of verses like Luke 4:23, but this precise phrase is not used in Scripture. It probably originated in a heading someone added to their New Testament or from a commentary or sermon. We've certainly seen the great healing power of Jesus in the first three chapters of Mark, so He definitely proved that He *is* a great physician. He repeatedly showed His power to cure fever, leprosy, paralysis, withered hands, and other diseases not mentioned.

But the key point is that when He miraculously healed people's bodies, He also forgave their sins. He said it's easy enough to *say*, "Your sins are forgiven," but how could He demonstrate that He had the power and authority to actually forgive people? They needed to *see* something.

So Jesus performed healing miracles to authenticate His power to forgive. That's exactly what He says in Mark 2:10-11: "'But *so that you may know* that the Son of Man has authority on earth to forgive sins'—He said to the paralytic, 'I say to you, get up, pick up your pallet and go home.'" Anyone can say, "Your sins are forgiven," but who can heal a paralytic? The One who healed the paralytic demonstrated an authority the people had never seen before.

Jesus had compassion on the sick. He healed them. He has compassion today and heals today. But the Gospels do not emphasize His ability to heal people of physical ailments. The compassion Jesus showed was toward the disease called *sin*, and He healed *that*. In doing so He proved that He was God, for only God can forgive sins. The scribes knew that, which is why they accused Him of blasphemy.

If we want to follow Jesus' example, we must show similar compassion toward the spiritually sick—people who are sinners. Only God can forgive sins, so we have to bring sinners to Him for healing. We must share the good news, the gospel of Jesus Christ, with sinners. If we focus on physical healing and miss the spiritual healing, we miss the point Jesus made. His healing miracles proved He was superior to Moses, the high priests, the Pharisees, the scribes, the rabbis, and everyone else of that day. The apostle Paul physically healed people too, but he did not focus on the healings. He focused on the gospel.

Likewise, our ministry today should not focus on physical healings, although those occur because God appointed "gifts of healings" (as opposed to healers) in His church (1 Corinthians 12:28), and people are thrilled to give Jesus the credit for them. When you consider our prayers, especially shared prayers, you notice that we often pray for this kind of healing. But how much more do we need to pray for spiritual healing? Physical illness distresses us; people suffer excruciatingly sometimes. And we pray for those we know are saved, whose sins have been forgiven, whose eternal destinies are secure. But how often do we pray for the lost—by name? Do we pray for our lost family members? What about neighbors, the people who go to school with us, and our coworkers? Do you suppose they are less distressed by spiritual torment than by physical suffering?

Jesus came to call sinners to repentance. How can we participate in this ministry?

He Who Has Ears to Hear, Let Him Hear

～～～～

God told Isaiah to deliver His message to Israel, but He warned him that the people would not receive it—they wouldn't have ears to hear. Until they were willing to turn from their wicked ways, the message would not penetrate their hearts. Jesus understood this, so when He came teaching parables, He explained them only to His disciples. Most of the people—especially the religious leaders—remained hard-hearted and were unable to accept His message.

～～～

DAY ONE

Greetings, steadfast student. And thank you for wanting to know your God better. As you begin this week of study, know that we're praying for you. Many people choose to spend their time on things other than the Word of God. They don't realize that they can meet God face-to-face by plumbing the depths of Holy Scripture. But you know it, and we're thankful for you. Press on this week, and don't let anything distract you from your devotion to our Lord.

Read Mark 4 today, marking key words and phrases, just as you have been doing for the past two weeks. Remember, marking gives you visual cues to repetition and the author's emphasis. That's how we see what the main ideas are. And keep asking those 5 W's and an H. Don't let your mind drift as you mark.

DAY TWO

Today we're going to continue our pattern. Now that we've read the chapter and marked key words, we want to go deeper into what God said in Mark 4. We'll list what we learned from each marking and see what God teaches us about Jesus. We'll ask questions that will help us know what He did, what He said, and how they relate.

This is an especially important text, so observe it carefully. Careful observation is a key to accurate interpretation and valid application.

DAY THREE

Mark mentioned parables in 3:23, but as you can see, parables are the most important topic in chapter 4. In fact, we'll see parables only twice more in Mark (chapters 7 and 12). The word *parable* comes from two Greek words meaning "to throw alongside." Parables illustrate or explain something that was previously unknown by comparing it with something that is known, something "thrown alongside," so to speak. The appendix of this book includes an article about parables that you'll want to read today to be sure that you accurately handle the Word of truth (2 Timothy 2:15).

Before we dig into each parable and determine its main

point, read Mark 4:10-12. These verses address the disciples' questions. Matthew 13:10 tells us one of their questions: "Why do you speak to them in parables?"

In Mark 4:12, Jesus quotes Isaiah 6:9-10. Read Isaiah 6 and compare verses 9-10 with Mark 4:12. What is the setting of Isaiah 6? What does God want Isaiah to do? How does Isaiah respond, and what is the result according to Isaiah 6:13?

How does this relate to Jesus' words in Mark 4:10-12? Read Mark 4:13,33-34.

What result does Jesus want? Is it the same thing God was looking for in Isaiah's day?

DAY FOUR

Mark 4 contains three parables involving seeds. They describe three different characteristics about the kingdom of God.

Read Mark 4:1-9 and note the four different kinds of soil the seed fell on. You can underline them, number them in the text, or both. In your notebook or wherever you're making your lists, make two columns. Label one column *Illustration,* and label the other one *Explanation.*

Use these columns to keep track of the points Jesus makes in each parable. For the parable of the sower, fill out the first column with the information you saw in verses 1-9.

Now read verses 14-20 and fill out the second column.

DAY FIVE

Today read Mark 4:21-29. The parable of the lamp in verses 21-25 is similar to something Jesus taught in the Sermon on the Mount. Read Matthew 5:14-16. Is the meaning clear?

Now mark verse 23 and then go back and mark the same phrase in verse 9 the same way.

Read Matthew 7:2, which is not as familiar to most people as Matthew 7:1. How does Mark 4:24 relate to Mark 4:21-23 and Matthew 7:2?

How does Mark 4:24-25 relate to Mark 4:10-13 and 33-34?

DAY SIX

Now read Mark 4:26-29. What does this second parable about seeds teach? Use your two-column chart to record the illustration and the explanation.

Read Mark 4:30-32. What are the illustration and the explanation?

What characteristic of the kingdom is Jesus describing in these two parables? Why is this important? Read Mark 1:15. Mark *kingdom of God* in a special way in Mark 1:15 and 4:26,30. Add this to your bookmark and watch for it in the rest of Mark.

In the remaining verses of Mark 4, the focus shifts from teaching to an event. What's the event, and what does it show about Jesus?

Determine a theme for Mark 4 and then record it on MARK AT A GLANCE in the appendix.

DAY SEVEN

 Store in your heart: Mark 4:20

Read and discuss: Mark 4

QUESTIONS FOR DISCUSSION OR INDIVIDUAL STUDY

- ∾ Start by reviewing the principles for interpreting parables. Be sure to let this guide your discussion of the parables so you don't ascribe meanings where texts are not clear.

- ∾ Also discuss the use of parables. According to Mark, why did Jesus teach in parables? Are the parables a meaningful way for you to embrace truth? Explain.

- ∾ Discuss the parable of the sower. What is the illustration, and what is the explanation? Describe each kind of soil. Which soil describes you the best?

- ∾ Discuss the illustrations and explanations contained in the other parables. What is the lamp?

- ∾ Who causes growth in the kingdom of God? Are you a sower?

- ∾ What happens to the tiny mustard seed? How does it compare to the kingdom of God?

- ∾ What is the significance of the event at the end of the chapter? What does Jesus ask His disciples? How would you answer His question if He asked you today?

THOUGHT FOR THE WEEK

In Jesus' day farmers in Israel scattered seed and then plowed it in. Today, like then, Galilee has very fertile soil which is also rocky with thistles growing everywhere. When Jesus told the parable of the sower, His audience was familiar with these soil features. They knew about seed thrown onto roads and into rocky soil and also how thorns and weeds grow up and choke what is planted. This was everyday life in agrarian Galilee 2000 years ago. It's much the same today.

And today, like then, many people don't understand the parable, even though they understand the illustration. They don't have ears to hear.

When we read Jesus' explanations of illustrations, we understand, but why is that? How is it that we have ears to hear? Jesus told His disciples that after He was gone He would send them the Helper, the Spirit of truth, who would guide them into all truth. The Spirit would help them understand the things Jesus said to them.

It is important to grasp the way the Holy Spirit helps us. We understand the parables of Jesus because the Holy Spirit is in us. The book of Acts clearly teaches that the Holy Spirit was not given just to the apostles or just to Jews who believed the gospel, but to all who believed, including Gentiles. The Holy Spirit guides all believers into all truth.

The three synoptic Gospels record many of Jesus' parables. They also record the explanations Jesus gave His disciples, but some questions remain. For example, in the first parable, do all four of the soils describe Christians, or do some of the soils represent non-Christians? If some are Christians and some are not, which soils represent which group of people?

And what about the results when the seeds are sown in these soils? If Satan snatches the word away from some people as soon as they have heard it, are these people unbelievers? What about those who receive the word with joy but then fall away when persecution arises—is Jesus talking about non-Christians? What about those who are unfruitful because the worries of the world, the deceitfulness of riches, and desires for other things choke out the good plants? What does their lack of fruit tell us?

John 15 shows that if people abide in Jesus, He will abide in them, and they will bear fruit. Conversely, those who do not abide in Jesus will not bear fruit—they are like dead branches that are thrown away and burned. According to 1 John 3:24, we know the Father abides in us because of the Spirit He gave us.

Therefore, we can conclude that only the last of the four soils, the good soil that produces fruit, represents Christians. These people will be judged at the judgment seat of Christ and rewarded for the fruit they have produced.

One of these rewards is the crown of life. All who persevere to the end receive this crown. Another is the crown of righteousness, which is awarded to all who have loved Jesus' appearing. And what do believers do with these crowns? If they follow the example of the 24 elders in Revelation, they cast their crowns toward the feet of Jesus in much the same way that the wise men gave gifts to Jesus when He was a toddler. The reason that those of us who abide in Jesus and produce good fruit will receive rewards in heaven is this: We will glorify God by giving our rewards back to Him, just as we glorify Him now by giving Him everything He has entrusted to us on this earth.

Good soil reflects the ability of the sower to care for the soil, and the ultimate Sower is the Son of Man (Matthew 13:37).

WHAT GREAT THINGS THE LORD HAS DONE FOR YOU

Mark has been telling us about the great things Jesus has done—healings, casting out demons, calming stormy seas. People were grateful for what He did, and they wanted others to know what happened. What about you? Do you want others to know what great things the Lord has done for you?

DAY ONE

Read Mark 5 and mark the key words from your bookmark. Be sure to mark the title for Jesus used in this chapter. You've seen it just a few times before. Don't forget to mark time phrases, like *immediately*, and geographical references.

DAY TWO

List what you learn from marking key words and phrases, asking the 5 W's and an H as you go. Be sure to note what you learn about the *unclean spirits* encountered here. Don't miss the importance of *faith*.

DAY THREE

Now read through the chapter again and mark off the three main subjects (stories or events) in the margin of your Bible. One is within another, so mark it in a way so that you can clearly see its beginning and end. Be sure to note the beginning and end of the "interrupted" story.

Now read Mark 4:35–5:1 as well as Mark 5:20. Is the story continued from one chapter to another? These stories are so central to demonstrating Jesus' power that all three appear in all three synoptic Gospels.

Remember, the sea that Mark refers to is the Sea of Galilee. The "other side" is another place on the shore. What is it called here? Check the map called "Regions from Which People Came to See Jesus" in the appendix to see where this is.

The Decapolis was a region of the Roman Empire with ten principal cities. In Greek, *deca* means "ten," and *polis* means "city." Most of these ten cities were on the east side of the Jordan River. Present-day Amman, Jordan, was one of these ten cities, but in those days the Romans called it Philadelphia.

What kind of animal does the first story include? Read Leviticus 11:1-8. What animal does Leviticus 11 mention that is also mentioned in Mark 5? What does this tell you about the people living in the country of the Gerasenes in the Decapolis? Remember that detail; we'll come back to it later.

DAY FOUR

Let's spend today on the first event in Mark 5. Note whom Jesus encounters, and list the details of what his life was like when Jesus met him. What's afflicting him? You have been listing what you are learning about demons (unclean spirits). How is this affliction different from what you have seen earlier in Mark?

What did the people of the region ask Jesus to do after the demons left the man and went into the swine? Compare this reaction to what you saw earlier in Mark. Why do you think people responded differently in this story?

What did Jesus tell the man who had the demons? Compare that with what He told people earlier in Mark. Why do you think Jesus said this to him?

DAY FIVE

Today we'll look at the second event in Mark 5. Remember, the whole story is in Mark 5:21-24,35-43. Read verses 21-22 to determine where the event takes place. How does this compare to the previous story?

Who comes to Jesus in this story, and what does he need? What does he believe about Jesus?

Jairus watched the events described in verses 25-34. What would Jairus have learned about faith from this event? What did he see? What did Jesus say to Jairus, the synagogue official, in verse 36?

How did the people react to Jesus' insistence that Jairus's daughter had not died but was just sleeping?

Whom did Jesus let accompany Him into the girl's room? What did He command the parents to do? Compare this to what Jesus said to the man who was possessed by a legion of demons.

Reflect on the lessons you learned from this story.

DAY SIX

Let's go back to the story in Mark 5:25-34. What was the woman's affliction? How was she healed?

How did Jesus respond to her faith? How did His disciples react? What do you learn about Jesus from this?

We have seen that Jesus displayed His power in a region where there were synagogues as well as in the Decapolis, where swine were raised. What does this tell you about Jesus' intention to reach people? Who is included? Read Romans 1:16-17.

Now what is the common theme of Mark 5? Or what are the main events of the chapter? Determine a theme for Mark 5 and record it on MARK AT A GLANCE.

DAY SEVEN

 Store in your heart: Mark 5:36
Read and discuss: Mark 5

QUESTIONS FOR DISCUSSION OR INDIVIDUAL STUDY

ᴄ Discuss the three events, being sure to cover the 5 W's and an H as you go.

- Where did these events occur?

- Who was involved?

- What afflictions did Jesus cure?

- How did Jesus deal with the affliction?

- How did the needy people react? Why?

- How did others around them react? Why?

- What command did Jesus give after He performed His miracles of healing?

- What do these stories reveal about Jesus?

∾ In these three stories, what three forces did Jesus prove His authority over? How important is this? When you couple this with the story toward the end of Mark 4, what do you see that Jesus has power over?

∾ What lessons for life did you learn from your study this week? How can you apply them to your life?

THOUGHT FOR THE WEEK

When anyone does something good for us, we are grateful and express that gratitude in our response.

In Mark 5, Jesus cast a legion of demons out of a man, healed a woman who had been bleeding for 12 years, and raised a young girl from the dead. He demonstrated His power over the demonic world (Satan and his workers), sickness, and death. As Jesus and His disciples were on the Sea of Galilee, Jesus revealed His power over the natural world—the wind and the waves. So Mark 5 shows us His power over the supernatural and natural worlds.

Are these separate worlds or one? Romans 6:23 says the wages of sin is death. Is this spiritual death, physical death, or both? Hebrews 2:14 tells us that the devil had the power of death. The truth is, physical death overcomes even those who have eternal life unless Jesus comes to take them away before they die (1 Thessalonians 4:13-18). But another truth is wrapped up in the story of Jairus's daughter: resurrection!

Jesus' resurrection is the key to eternal life. Jesus died

on the cross, but He also rose from the dead. It's not enough to speak of His atoning blood, which was shed on the cross for the forgiveness of sins. That's truth, but it's not the whole truth. First Corinthians 15:21-22 teaches that death came to all men because of Adam. But life comes because of Christ's resurrection. Those who have "fallen asleep in Christ" may be physically dead, as Jairus's daughter was, but Jesus guarantees their resurrection.

That's what 1 Thessalonians 4:13-18 teaches. There Paul talks about those who have "fallen asleep in Jesus Christ," whom he also calls the "dead in Christ." People who are "in Christ" may be physically dead, but from the point of view of eternal life, their bodies are only asleep. Jesus will wake them at His coming, just as He did that little 12-year-old girl.

The difference, though, is that when the little girl "woke up," nothing about her changed. Her body was just as it had been before she got sick. First Corinthians 15 makes clear that at the last resurrection, our earthly bodies will be raised in power and transformed into spiritual bodies that will be imperishable and immortal—just like Christ's resurrection body. The story of the little girl only illustrates Christ's power over death and gives us a hint that those who are "asleep in Christ" will be raised.

From this story in Mark 5, we have proof that Jesus wakes those who are "asleep in Christ." So when Paul teaches about the resurrection of those "asleep in Christ," should we take his words literally? Based on what evidence?

And what do we do with this truth? Do we keep it to ourselves, or do we tell others? What did Paul do? If we're grateful for this truth, how do we thank Jesus? Do we do so by keeping it to ourselves or by sharing it? If we know from the record of these three events that Jesus has complete control over both the natural and the supernatural realms, what is the appropriate response?

I like to think that we would be as grateful as the demon-possessed man in the country of the Gerasenes. Before Jesus released us from the grip of Satan, we were like that man. And now we are like the man released from the legion of demons. But do we proclaim what great things Jesus has done for us? Maybe our story isn't quite so dramatic. But it is identical in that we were in the grip of Satan but now are in our "right minds," clothed in the righteousness of Christ. Aren't you grateful? Tell someone this week what great things Jesus has done for you.

How Do These Events Fit Together?

Studying the events in Jesus' earthly ministry and understanding them separately can yield wonderful results, but that alone isn't enough. The events are connected; they fit together to tell a larger story. Jesus' own disciples didn't make the connections. Can you? That's why we do inductive study, Beloved! It's the best way to make those connections.

DAY ONE

Begin your study today with prayer, asking the Father to help you see how the elements of Mark 6 fit together so you can better understand Jesus' message. Read the chapter and mark the key words on your bookmark. Also mark references to the main characters of the story about John the Baptist, but don't add these to your bookmark.

DAY TWO

Read Mark 6 again and mark the events in the margin of your Bible. From each story, list what you learn from your markings. Be sure to note references to time and locations.

DAY THREE

Note the location of the first story in Mark 6. Read Mark 3:20-21,31 again. What was Jesus' hometown? How do you know from the context of this story? What do you learn about His family?

Note what Jesus does and when. List the reactions of the people. How does Jesus respond to them?

DAY FOUR

The second event in Mark 6 is described in verses 7-12 and also in verse 30. What happens? Who is involved? List the specific instructions Jesus gave His disciples. What principles underlie them?

What message did the disciples give, and what were their deeds? How does this compare to what Jesus was doing?

The parallel passage in Matthew 10 gives some interesting details. Read Matthew 10:1-23, noting the important things you learn.

DAY FIVE

Read Mark 1:4-15 and then 6:14-29. Note how the two episodes relate. Review the events in Mark 6 about John the Baptist and note why Herod imprisoned John.

Look at the chart called "Herod's Family Tree" in the appendix. Find Herodias and then find Herod Antipas and Herod Philip to see their relationships. Also find the Herod and Archelaus mentioned in Matthew 2:19-23. This family of Herod the Great plays important roles in the Gospels and Acts.

In 6 BC, while still in her infancy, Herodias was betrothed by her grandfather, Herod the Great, to his son by Mariamne II named Herod Philip. Herodias was the mother of Salome, born between AD 15 and 19.

In AD 29, Herod Antipas visited Herodias' (his niece) residence on his way to Rome. They were attracted to each other, and Herodias agreed to marry him provided he would divorce his present wife, the daughter of Aretas IV, the Arabian king of Petra. Herodias, a Hasmonean, did not want to share the house with an Arab—longtime foes of the Hasmonean dynasty. When Aretas' daughter got word of this plot, she secretly escaped to her father; and Herodias and Antipas were married. John the Baptist openly denounced this marriage because Jewish law forbade marriage with one's brother's wife except in order to raise children for a deceased childless brother by a levirate marriage. In this case the brother, Herod Philip, was still alive and had a child, Salome.*

If you want to see for yourself what the Old Testament says about this, read Leviticus 18:16; 20:21 and Deuteronomy 25:5-6.

DAY SIX

Read Mark 6:31-44. Note Jesus' reaction to the crowd and His disciples' reaction to His directive to them. How did Jesus demonstrate His power here?

---

* W.A. Elwell and B.J. Beitzel, *Baker Encyclopedia of the Bible* (Grand Rapids: Baker Book House, 1988), 973.

Now read Mark 6:45-52. What is the connection between the two stories? Underline or mark the phrases that tell you. What have the people not learned? What about you? Have you learned what Jesus expected the 12 to understand?

Finally, what are the last four verses of Mark 6 about? What is the main principle, and how does it relate to the other events?

Finally, determine a theme for Mark 6 and record it on MARK AT A GLANCE.

DAY SEVEN

 Store in your heart: Mark 6:50 (just what Jesus said to the disciples in the boat)
Read and discuss: Mark 6

QUESTIONS FOR DISCUSSION OR INDIVIDUAL STUDY

- Discuss your insights about Jesus' hometown's reaction to His teaching.

- Discuss His commands to the 12 disciples and the results of their journeys.

- Discuss the story of Herod and John the Baptist. What insights do you have about the consequences of speaking truth?

- Discuss the feeding of the 5000. What should the disciples have learned from this event?

- What happened on the boat, and what insights do you have?

- What applications can you make from Mark 6?

THOUGHT FOR THE WEEK

After Jesus fed the 5000, John's Gospel records that Jesus said the people sought Him because of the meal. Their stomachs were full; their physical needs were met. They were following Jesus for reasons of self-interest and expediency, not for spiritual reasons.

John also records a teaching that neither Matthew, Mark, nor Luke record: Jesus is the bread of life. The people's satisfied appetites gave Jesus an opportunity to teach a spiritual truth by comparing them to the Israelites who wandered in the wilderness after their exodus from Egypt. In that wilderness, God fed manna to Israel for 40 years. Each morning it appeared on the ground, and the people gathered enough for that day.

> Then the Lord said to Moses, "Behold, I will rain bread from heaven for you; and the people shall go out and gather a day's portion every day, that I may test them, whether or not they will walk in My instruction" (Exodus 16:4).

The Israelites filled their stomachs with manna, but eventually they got tired of it and complained that they had no meat. They never saw beyond the physical sustenance to the God who provided it for them.

Jesus taught His listeners to look to heaven for the bread that comes down and gives eternal life. Bread sustained their physical lives, but faith in the promised seed of Abraham gives eternal life. Jesus likened Himself to the manna, the bread that came down from heaven and gave life. But His hearers didn't understand what He meant. They didn't understand that He was talking about hungering and thirsting for righteousness, which is satisfied only by coming to Him through faith.

Similarly, here in Mark, the disciples didn't understand the meaning of Jesus' feeding the 5000. Verse 52 says "they had not gained any insight from the incident of the loaves, for their heart was hardened."

Later, when Jesus came to them walking on water, they were terrified. He spoke to them and got into the boat, and they were amazed. But still they did not believe. Just as Jesus told His listeners in the Gospel of John, they saw Him but did not believe.

An old proverb says, "Seeing is believing." Missouri is the "Show me" state. Skeptics, echoing Thomas, say, "I won't believe it until I see it with my own eyes." The problem with Jesus' audience is that they saw with *physical* eyes but not *spiritual* ones; they did not believe. And it's not surprising because what they saw was unbelievable. Today we're accustomed to illusionists' sleight of hand, so we have a hard time believing what we see (or think we see). We're jaded by lies, half-truths, deception, and spin, so we have an especially hard time believing what we're told.

Sometimes we read about the bad reactions of the disciples in the Gospels and assume we'd be different. But the sin nature we share with them tells us otherwise. Jesus' assessment that they were "slow to believe" (Luke 24:25) would certainly have applied to us as well. Why? Because a factor is involved that's not a matter of self-effort. Jesus put it this way in John 6:44: "No one can come to Me, unless the Father who sent Me draws him."

We can see; we can hear. But what does it take to believe? The Father must draw us.

WHO DO YOU SAY JESUS IS?

In Jesus' day, some people thought He was Elijah, others believed He was John the Baptist, and still others were convinced He was one of the prophets. In the first few centuries of Christianity, some people thought Jesus was just a man and that the Christ was an independent spirit that descended on Him at His baptism and abandoned Him when He died. Today, some people, even some who call themselves Christians, think Jesus was merely a good man, a moral teacher, or a prophet. But who is He really? What do You say? What does the Bible say?

DAY ONE

We're going to cover two chapters this week as we did in week 2, so the pace will be a little more rapid than in other weeks. Read Mark 7 today, marking the key words from your bookmark. Mark *tradition* but don't add it to your bookmark. It appears only in this chapter. Also mark *if anyone has ears to hear, let him hear* [4] as you did in Mark 4. This phrase appears in brackets in the NASB because it isn't found in early manuscripts.

53

DAYS TWO & THREE

Read through Mark 7 again. Mark the events and note whom Jesus is among. What's the big issue with the Pharisees and scribes? What does Jesus teach?

If you would like more information on the Pharisees, read Matthew 16:1-12 and Luke 18:9-14.

Did you notice that Mark explains the customs of the Jews? This is one of the reasons many commentators believe Mark was writing to Gentiles.

What is the significance of verses 18-19? Isn't this teaching contrary to the Law? What is Jesus' point?

In your remaining study time, list what you learn from marking key words. Don't forget to record a theme for Mark 7 on MARK AT A GLANCE.

DAY FOUR

Now read Mark 8, marking the key words from your bookmark as usual. Also mark *sign* and add it to your bookmark.

DAY FIVE

Read Mark 8 again, and in the margin of your Bible, note the main events. Also note locations as usual.

Compare the first event with the one in Mark 6:34-44. Note the two stories' similarities and differences. Read Mark 7:31 again. Where is Jesus? What does this tell you about the people Jesus fed in the two accounts?

Read Matthew 16:1-4 and Luke 11:29-32. What detail

does Mark leave out in the second event? Remember, if we're correct that Mark is addressing Gentiles, then Old Testament characters and events don't contribute to his purpose. Luke adds details neither Matthew nor Mark include.

DAY SIX

The event that occurs in Caesarea Philippi in Mark 8:27-33 is one of the most important in the book. Think back over the first seven chapters. What have the people called Jesus? What have the demons called Him? Finally, what does Peter call Him here, and how did Peter get this knowledge? Read Matthew 16:13-17.

Notice what Jesus now tells His disciples after Peter confesses who He really is. Also note Peter's reaction and Jesus' response to Peter.

What main point does Jesus teach in verses 34-38? Much of Mark focuses on events, but here Jesus teaches truth that is critical for all Christians.

Finally, record a theme for Mark 8 on MARK AT A GLANCE.

DAY SEVEN

 Store in your heart: Mark 8:29
Read and discuss: Mark 7–8

QUESTIONS FOR DISCUSSION OR INDIVIDUAL STUDY

- ∾ Compare and contrast the feeding of the 4000 with the feeding of the 5000. Did they have the same purpose? Explain your answer.

- ∾ Discuss Jesus' confrontation with the Pharisees and scribes in both chapters. What are the main points?

- ∾ Discuss the role traditions play in your personal life and in your church. How do your traditions help you obey God? How do they hinder you?

- ∾ What is the significance and application of Jesus declaring all foods clean? Discuss what defiles a person.

- ∾ Discuss Peter's confession of Jesus as the Christ. Compare what Jesus called Himself with what others called Him.

- ∾ What did Jesus mean when He said His followers must take up his cross? What is your cross, and how can you take it up?

THOUGHT FOR THE WEEK

"You are the Christ," Peter declared at Caesarea Philippi. Some call this statement the Great Confession, holding it up alongside the Great Commission (making disciples in the entire world—Matthew 28:18-20) and the Great Commandment (loving God with the whole heart, soul, mind, and strength—Matthew 22:36). These three "great" statements mark important facets of the Christian faith— believing Jesus is the Son of God, obeying Him by making disciples, and loving God completely. This isn't an exhaustive list, but it does make three good headings to cover the major aspects.

Some people thought Jesus was John the Baptist, and others thought He was Elijah, Jeremiah, or another prophet, but Peter stated the truth. According to Matthew's Gospel, Peter added that Jesus is also the Son of the living God. Jesus responded that Peter was blessed to have recognized Him because God, not man, revealed Jesus' true nature to him.

Herod thought Jesus was John the Baptist, who he thought had come back from the dead. Later, Jesus will explain that John was Elijah the forerunner, the one who prepared the way for Jesus. A great deal of speculation had been going on, but God revealed the truth to Peter. And from that moment on, Jesus explained much to the disciples that He hadn't told them before, because the stage was now set.

The Pharisees, the scribes, the Sadducees, and others wanted to see signs that validated Jesus' messianic authority. If people were going to follow Jesus, they wanted to know He was from God. So Jesus began to teach what it means to follow Him.

Even the disciples didn't fully understand and believe God's purpose in sending His Son, the Messiah, to die. Peter feared the idea of His suffering and dying because he didn't understand and grasp the significance of Jesus' death and resurrection. The disciples didn't realize that Jesus had to return to the Father. All this was yet to be revealed to Jesus' disciples.

So who do you think Jesus is? Are you convinced He is who He says He is? If so, you must take to heart what Jesus says at the end of Mark 8 about being a disciple. Are you ready to lose your life, to surrender it all to Jesus, to defend the faith and maintain your testimony? Many do today. They're called martyrs. They give witness to the truth of the gospel and testify about its value.

What's at stake when you defend the faith? What's at stake when you are willing to die rather than deny Christ? Your immortal soul! Jesus asks what profit it is for you to gain the whole world but lose your soul in the process. Whether you believe Jesus or not, you can't take the world's products with you when you die.

When John D. Rockefeller died in 1937, someone reportedly asked how much he left behind. The answer was simple: all of it. (For the curious, it was about $900 million, or $13 billion in today's dollars.)

The point is that you take nothing with you. Why chase after things you can't keep at the risk of losing your soul? What is the most valuable thing you have if it isn't your soul? And which is more valuable—things that are temporal, that exist in this world, or things that are eternal? Your worldly possessions are temporal; your soul is eternal. Even if you were richer than Warren Buffett or Bill Gates, if you owned the entire world, your riches would still be temporary, and your soul would still be eternal. What's at stake is where your eternal soul spends eternity—with God or in the lake of fire.

Is Hell Real?

If you ask people today if they think they'll go to heaven when they die, you usually get one of four answers: yes, no, I hope so, or I don't believe in heaven. Those who give the last answer usually don't believe in God at all. Some are nihilists, who reject any afterlife. Others believe in reincarnation. Those who give the second answer may be convinced of their evil behavior yet have no fear of hell. The third answer comes from those who think entrance into heaven is based on behavior; they just don't know whether they're good enough to pass the test. Those who answer yes believe either everyone goes to heaven or only some. But regardless of these ideas about who goes to heaven, only one question has eternal significance for you, and it's this: Will *you* go to heaven or hell when you die? What can matter more to you than your personal eternal destiny?

DAY ONE

Spend your study time today observing Mark 9 and marking the words on your bookmark. Note or mark in a special way the key people in this chapter. Mark *stumble* and *discuss* but do not add them to your bookmark.

DAY TWO

Now list what you learned from marking the key words and people in Mark 9. Mark key events and teachings in the margin of your Bible.

DAY THREE

Review the events around Mark 4:40; 6:50; and 9:6, all of which produced fear in the disciples. Compare the disciples' reaction to the event in each passage. The Greek word translated *afraid* in Mark 4:40 is *deilos*, meaning cowardly, or timid. Mark 6:50 contains two words: first, the word translated *terrified* is from the Greek verb *tarasso*, which means troubled, or agitated, implying doubt; second, Jesus' command, "Do not be *afraid*" uses the Greek verb *phobeo*. Finally, 9:6 has *ekphobeo* for *terrified*, a strengthened form of *phobeo* meaning great fear, which the King James Version translates "sore afraid."

What would make the disciples more afraid at the transfiguration than at the previous events?

Now compare Mark 9:7 with Mark 1:11. What do you learn?

Why did the disciples ask the question in Mark 9:11?

Read Matthew 11:1-14 and Malachi 3:10; 4:5. Compare these to Mark 9:11-13.

What were the disciples discussing? What don't they understand? Read Mark 8:31-33.

DAY FOUR

What is the main event in Mark 9:14-29? Review your lists from day 1 about the people: disciples, scribes, the crowd, and the father.

Carefully compare Mark 9:23-24 with verse 19. What does Jesus say the problem is? What does this reveal about the crowd, the scribes, and the father?

What does Mark 9:28-29 reveal about the disciples?

Now read Matthew 17:14-21. What additional insights do you gain?

DAYS FIVE & SIX

Read Mark 9:30-32. What did the disciples not understand? How did they feel about their ignorance? Remember what you saw in Mark 8:31-33 and 9:9-10.

How do you feel when you don't understand something in Scripture? Do you react like these disciples? Read 1 John 4:18 and Hebrews 4:16. Remember that you have a resident Teacher, the Holy Spirit, to call on.

What were the disciples discussing in the final event of this chapter? How did Jesus explain the answer to their question?

Review your lists about the main characters. How does the example of the children relate to Jesus' answer about first and last? Read Matthew 18:1-10 for additional insight.

Now, what is the main point of Jesus' teaching about stumbling and stumbling blocks? What causes someone to stumble?

From this teaching, what do you learn about hell and

the kingdom of God? What is the evidence that hell is real?
Read Isaiah 66:21-24.

Record a theme for Mark 9 on MARK AT A GLANCE.

DAY SEVEN

Store in your heart: Mark 9:37

Read and discuss: Mark 9

QUESTIONS FOR DISCUSSION OR INDIVIDUAL STUDY

- ∾ Discuss what you learned from the transfiguration.

    - What is the significance of what God said?

    - What does the reaction of the disciples mean?

    - What is the importance of Elijah, and how does he relate to John the Baptist?

- ∾ Discuss the healing of the boy with the unclean spirit and how belief and prayer were involved.

- ∾ Discuss the 12 disciples' progressive understanding of the resurrection. (Include what you learned earlier in Mark.)

- ∾ What do "first" and "last" in the kingdom of God mean?

- ∾ How can we apply Jesus' teaching about stumbling and causing people to stumble?

- ∾ What does Jesus teach about hell?

- ∾ What additional applications can you make from this chapter?

THOUGHT FOR THE WEEK

Some sophisticates today sneer at the idea of hell. Others who acknowledge that it's real deny that anyone ends up there. They focus only on God's love and doubt that a loving God can send anyone to hell. In their view, everyone goes to heaven because of God's love and mercy. That's a sweet sentiment and so encouraging, but is it true?

When people teach that God is good, that everything is going to turn out all right, and that there is no alternative to heaven, does their teaching agree with Scripture? Does this reflect a biblical view of redemption? What did Jesus teach?

In Mark 9, Jesus equates entering life (verse 43) with entering the kingdom of God (verse 47). That He's equating the two is evident by the fact that He's speaking to people already alive on earth. And so He's speaking of a future state that involves both spiritual life—the life of the soul—and a kingdom. Remember that in Mark 8, Jesus said the one who wishes to save his life will lose it, but the one who loses his life for His sake will save it. There, the soul was the issue, not the material body or the things of this world.

In Mark 9, this idea of what is more important—the material things of this earth or the spiritual things of the kingdom of God—is explained in a more dramatic way. Losing possessions is an unhappy event. Losing life is a full commitment. Cutting off a hand or foot or plucking out an eye is a sacrifice that is motivated by the reality of hell. But if everyone enters the kingdom of God, as some people believe, what Jesus says here makes no sense. If everyone enters life, Jesus wouldn't need to talk about sacrificing life or limb to avoid hell.

Eternal life in heaven and eternal punishment in hell are both taught in Scripture. They are two destinations, two outcomes, based on two distinctly different choices. You can choose the world and forfeit heaven. But if you forfeit heaven, you receive hell. No third option exists.

In Isaiah 66:24, the prophet describes a scene in which those who bow down before God will "go forth and look on the corpses of men who have transgressed against [God]." Then he says, "Their worm will not die and their fire will not be quenched." Jesus Himself quotes this phrase. The Greek word translated *hell* in Mark 9 is *gehenna*. South of Jerusalem is Ben Hinnom (that is, the valley of Hinnom), where animal carcasses and refuse were dumped to be burned. The two books of Kings, 1 and 2 Chronicles, and Jeremiah all describe how even the Israelites at times offered their children as burned sacrifices to the pagan god Molech in this valley. This child sacrifice to an idol was an abomination to God and part of the reason He judged Israel. Isaiah says the corpses of these transgressors "will be an abhorrence to all mankind."

Revelation 20 describes the lake of fire as the eternal destination of Satan, the beast, the false prophet, death and Hades, and all whose names are not written in the book of life. The beast and false prophet are thrown alive into this fire, where Satan eventually joins them and they are tormented day and night forever and ever. This lake of fire is also called the second death, and it's as eternal as eternal life. Surely this is what Isaiah meant. Surely this is what Jesus meant. Surely it is real.

So the next time someone mentions "hellfire and damnation" preaching in a way that belittles or denigrates the reality of hell, remember what God says. People jokingly refer to faith in God as "fire insurance." It's not. Salvation is not fire insurance, but life itself. Fire insurance pays you money if your possessions burn up. It doesn't pay you anything when you die in the fire; the money goes to your estate, which your heirs receive. But the heirs of salvation receive "the water of life without cost" from God Himself.

Don't let people make fun of hell, intimidate you into believing hell is false, or tell you to avoid talking about it. Without eternal life, hell is certain. The truth is a matter of life and death.

THE FIRST SHALL BE LAST

Many people's lives are filled with self-interest, as we see in phrases like these: *That's mine, you're on your own, it's every man for himself, me first,* and *watch out for number one.* This is the natural cry of children and adults whom the Bible describes as depraved. It reflects our human nature, the flesh we're born with. Babies are the perfect example— their focus is on their own needs and desires from the get-go. But the Bible reveals that life is not primarily about us. It's about God. Jesus had to teach His disciples this principle, and we need to hear it today.

DAY ONE

Read Mark 10, marking key words from your bookmark. We find a new title for Jesus in this chapter; watch for it and note who calls Him by this title. Keeping track of references to locations will help you follow the story. Events in Mark have not been strictly chronological up to now, but from here to the end they will be.

DAY TWO

Following our pattern, go through the chapter and mark the events in the margin of your Bible. Sometimes you'll see a key repeated word in just one event. If you do and you want to mark it, go ahead. It's your decision. These are flexible principles to help you observe. Some people mark more words than other people do.

Next, list what you learn from marking the key words.

DAY THREE

Now let's start examining the events in Mark 10 to see what key principles we can extract. Read verses 1-12. What is the key topic? Who questioned Jesus, why, and what was the subject?

How did Jesus respond? What had the Pharisees not understood? What did the disciples not understand?

Matthew 19:1-9 is a parallel passage. And Paul wrote the Corinthian church about divorce as well, answering questions they had asked. Read 1 Corinthians 7:10-16. For a more complete study, try *A Marriage Without Regrets* by Kay Arthur (Harvest House Publishers) or the *Marriage Without Regrets* Precept Upon Precept Bible Study (Precept Ministries International), both available by calling Precept Ministries at (800) 763-8280 or by visiting www.precept.org.

DAY FOUR

Read Mark 10:13-16. Compare what is said about children to what you saw last week in Mark 9:35-42. What principles do you see illustrated in the example of children?

Now read Mark 10:17-27. What's the question in verse 17? What did the disciples ask in verse 26? What phrase did Jesus use in verses 23-25? What does "enter the kingdom of God" mean?

Why did Jesus tell the wealthy man to sell his possessions? Are possessions evil? What was the man's attitude toward his possessions? What is your attitude toward your possessions?

DAY FIVE

Read Mark 10:28-31. How do these verses relate to the previous section? Now read Mark 10:32-40. How do verses 28-31 bridge between the section about how hard it is to enter the kingdom and the next section?

What are James and John asking, and what are they claiming they can do? Note Jesus' response to James and John. What will happen to them? What is the "baptism" they will share with Jesus? Compare Mark 9:35 with 10:31 and 10:42-45. In what ways are you choosing to serve rather than be served?

DAY SIX

Read Mark 10:46-52. List what you learn about Bartimaeus. What did he call Jesus? Compare this event with Jesus' healing of a blind man in Mark 8:22-25. What progression do you see in Mark 8:22-25?

Now read Isaiah 42:1-7. How can you relate to being blind and then seeing?

Well, that's it for this week, Beloved! Don't forget to record a theme for Mark 10 on MARK AT A GLANCE.

DAY SEVEN

Store in your heart: Mark 10:31
Read and discuss: Mark 10

QUESTIONS FOR DISCUSSION OR INDIVIDUAL STUDY

- What have you learned about divorce in your study of Mark? Remember, there is more to the issue than what you found in these brief passages.

- According to Jesus, what can children teach us about entering the kingdom of God?

- What did you learn from the story of the wealthy man about eternal life, the kingdom of God, and being saved?

- Discuss this principle: "Many who are first will be last, and the last, first."

- What did Jesus mean by "the cup that I drink" and "the baptism with which I am baptized"? Did the disciples drink this cup? Did they receive this baptism? They said they were able to do these things. Do you believe you are able?

- What principles did you learn from the healing of Bartimaeus?

- Contrast James and John's answer to Jesus' question (10:39) with Bartimaeus's (10:51).

THOUGHT FOR THE WEEK

In the well-known hymn "Amazing Grace," we sing, "I once...was blind but now I see." Jesus healed the blind man Bartimaeus on the road from Jericho to Jerusalem. That road ascends from below sea level in the Jordan River valley to the mountainous ridge that Jerusalem sits on. Jesus and His disciples were ascending to Jerusalem, to the holy mountain of God for the feast of Passover. God had commanded His people to go to Jerusalem three times a year to celebrate the feasts He appointed.

Passover marks the beginning of the Hebrew year (spring), when new life springs up from the ground. It also marks the exodus of the nation of Israel from slavery in Egypt to freedom in the land God promised to Abraham. The Old Testament metaphorically describes this land as flowing with milk and honey.

When Moses sent 12 spies into the land, they saw how fertile it was, but they couldn't see how God could give it to them. They were blind to His power. That generation did not have eyes of faith, so they never saw the Promised Land even though they had seen the power of God again and again in their wilderness wanderings. They had physical eyes, but they didn't have spiritual eyes to see and ears to hear (Deuteronomy 29:4).

In contrast to this, Bartimaeus lacked physical sight, but he had spiritual sight because he recognized Jesus as the Son of David. *Son of David* is a messianic title acknowledging that the promised deliverer would be a descendant of King David. By the time of Jesus, no descendant of David had ruled on the throne of Israel for 600 years. God's people longed for the Messiah, but although they physically saw Jesus, they had no spiritual insight—they couldn't see that

Jesus was the promised Messiah. But this blind man with no physical sight saw who Jesus was.

How much like the Jews are we? Can we see physical things but not spiritual ones? Are we blind to the spiritual things around us? Do we see the visible world but not the invisible Creator? Do we see physical life and death but remain blind to the spiritual life-and-death struggle around us?

Jesus explained physical death and physical resurrection. His disciples grasped the literal meaning of His words, but they couldn't grasp the spiritual significance. Peter confessed that Jesus was the Christ, the Son of God, but neither he nor the rest of the 12 disciples grasped the spiritual significances of the two titles. They weren't physically blind like Bartimaeus, but they couldn't see these spiritual truths.

We need to remember that we couldn't see them either until Jesus gave us sight. Physical sight is not enough. We need spiritual sight; we need to believe. Only then do we see Jesus in the way the Father intended—as our Savior, our Redeemer, our Messiah. And we need to remember that Jesus gives us that sight. That should make us humble enough to be happy with being last, not first.

BLESSED IS THE COMING KINGDOM OF OUR FATHER DAVID

Old Testament prophecies spoke of a Messiah descending from David, sitting on his throne, and reestablishing his family's rule over Israel. Now Jesus, David's descendant, comes riding into Jerusalem to shouts of acclamation. Did the people understand who was riding the donkey and why?

DAY ONE

This week we'll study Mark 11. As usual, start with careful observation, marking the key words from your bookmark. Don't forget to mark references to location and time.

DAY TWO

List what you learn from marking the key words in Mark 11. Then note in the margin of your Bible the key events. You can find them easily by noting time references.

DAY THREE

Let's look carefully at the first scene, which is in verses 1-10. On what did Jesus ride into Jerusalem?

Read John 12:12-18 and note the additional details John gives. The animal Jesus chose signified His intent. Read Zechariah 9:9 to determine Jesus' intent and what the people could have recognized if they had remembered this verse.

The greeting the people gave Jesus was typical for a noted visitor at a Passover. According to John, why did so many people turn out to greet Jesus? From Mark 11:10, why are they greeting Him? What kingdom are they looking for?

DAY FOUR

Read Mark 11:11-14,20-26. Although Mark does not identify this story as a parable, Jesus had a point beyond eating figs. Note the key words in Mark 11:20-26. What point was Jesus making? What's the connection between faith and prayer?

Read Matthew 6:9-15 and compare it with Mark 11:25-26. What do these passages teach about the connection between prayer and forgiveness?

Don't take these verses in Mark out of context. There's much more in the Bible about prayer. Also read 1 John 5:14, James 4:3, 1 Peter 3:7, and Isaiah 59:2. What do you learn? If you want to study prayer more thoroughly, get a copy of *Lord, Teach Me to Pray in 28 Days* from Precept Ministries International at www.precept.org or (800) 763-8280.

DAY FIVE

Read Mark 11:15-19 again. Compare these verses with Isaiah 56:7 and Jeremiah 7:11. The Jews needed to convert Roman currency into something acceptable to pay the temple tax because Roman coins with images of Caesar were considered unclean. And instead of bringing doves from their homes, they customarily bought doves in Jerusalem. What kind of atmosphere do you think the temple took on with all these commercial activities?

Also, the temple was on the east side of Jerusalem, near the Mount of Olives. Because a bridge and gate into the city were nearby, merchants used the temple as a shortcut on their way to do business. How does this help make verse 16 clear? Are you beginning to understand Jesus' response to all this in verses 15 and 16?

DAY SIX

Read Mark 11:27-33 again to review its content. Who challenges Jesus and how? Why did they ask this question? How did Jesus respond? Why did He refuse to answer them directly?

Think back over the first ten chapters of Mark. What kind of relationship did Jesus have with the leading officials of Israel? Why? If you don't recall, look at these passages:

Mark 3:1-6

Mark 3:20-22

Mark 7:1-13

Mark 8:11-12

Mark 10:2-9

Record a theme for Mark 11 on MARK AT A GLANCE.

DAY SEVEN

Store in your heart: Mark 11:25
Read and discuss: Mark 11

QUESTIONS FOR DISCUSSION OR INDIVIDUAL STUDY

- Discuss what you learned about Jesus' entrance into Jerusalem.

- What principles of prayer did you learn this week? How can you apply them to your life?

- What was God's intention for the temple? What problem did Jesus address when He cleared out the money changers and dove sellers? Can we apply this in any way today?

- Review what you learned in Mark about Jesus' authority. What is the source of His authority? What does He have authority over? Who challenged Jesus' authority? What did they challenge?

- What difference does Mark 11 make in your life? What truths in this chapter speak to issues in your life?

THOUGHT FOR THE WEEK

Jesus cleared the merchants out of the temple because they were perverting its purpose. God designed the temple to be a house of prayer for all nations, but it became a place of commerce, worldly and man-centered. Prayer is God-centered.

In the Sermon on the Mount, Jesus taught His disciples

not to pray like hypocrites, who loved to stand and pray in public so they could be seen by men. They wanted people to think they were holy, spiritual, close to God. But Jesus explained that they were far from God. He said human acknowledgment of their behavior was the only reward they would get.

And He taught that in contrast with the hypocrites, those who prayed to the Father in secret would receive a reward from the Father. Secret prayer is God-centered, not man-centered. God sees what man cannot. People's opinion of your prayers and even their awareness that you pray are unimportant. God rewards people who pray to Him without hypocrisy.

Jesus also taught that God does not respond to the meaningless repetition in Gentiles' prayers because He knows what people need before they ask.

The Lord's Prayer demonstrates some important principles. Notice that the prayer begins with a statement of the Father's value—His name is holy. Next comes a pledge of allegiance to God's rule in heaven and on earth. Then we see requests that imply that God is the One who provides for both physical and spiritual needs.

The prayer requests forgiveness "as we also have forgiven our debtors." It assumes that true believers have forgiven others and asks for similar treatment. In Mark 11 we see the same teaching—whenever we pray, we are to make sure that we forgive others so that our Father in heaven will forgive our sins.

Matthew 18:21-22 records a conversation in which Peter asks Jesus a question about forgiving others. He asks how many times he should forgive. Jesus answers, "Seventy times seven." Jesus follows this with an analogy of forgiveness, likening forgiveness to releasing a debt. Given the size of the debt we owe God, His forgiveness has to be great. When people do things that require our forgiveness, we could forgive 490 times ("seventy times seven") and not come close to matching the forgiveness we receive from God.

So the principle is clear. The Father will not answer our prayers if we don't forgive others, because His forgiveness is far greater. We cannot expect Him to grant our request if we cannot grant others even a tiny fraction of the grace He has given us. We *ask* the Father for grace. We don't come to Him demanding what we have earned, because we know we've earned death, the wages of sin. We ask because we rely on God's grace. If we don't extend the grace of forgiveness to others, we prove that we have not truly received God's grace. If we don't forgive others from our hearts, God's forgiveness hasn't found a place in us.

And only God can forgive our sins.

TESTING THE TRUTH

Don't you just hate tests? Most people do. Tests scare us. But they're necessary to discover truth. Medical tests are used to discover what's wrong. Driving tests are used to see if you know how to drive. School tests are used to show what you've learned. Metals are tested to see how pure they are. But the Pharisees and other religious leaders used tests for their own purposes: to trap Jesus and gain an advantage over Him. But when the truth is tested, what result do you expect?

DAY ONE

Read Mark 12 today, marking the key words from your bookmark and asking the 5 W's and an H. Mark distinctively each person who questioned Jesus, but don't add them to your bookmark.

DAY TWO

Today, mark the events in Mark 12 in the margin of your Bible and then list in your notebook what you learned from each. What life principles can you find? What good and bad examples lie before us? What truths about God can stir us up to action?

DAY THREE

Now let's look more closely at the parable in Mark 12:1-12. Read from Mark 11:27 through Mark 12:12 again and identify the characters in the parable. Read Isaiah 5:1-2 and then use it and Mark 12:12 as clues to identify the man who planted the vineyard, the vineyard, the vine-growers, the slaves, and the son. It's not difficult. Just piece together what you've studied before. Now, what's the main point of the parable? Remember, every parable has a main point.

DAY FOUR

Today let's tackle the first group of questioners. Read Mark 12:13-17 and identify who is asking questions, what the questions are, what the motive is, and how Jesus counters the challenges to His authority.

Pharisees were the largest religious sect of Jews in Jesus' day, dating from about 150 BC. The word *Pharisee* means "separated one." Pharisees separated themselves from the influences of Hellenism, or the Greek way of living at the time. Most scribes were Pharisees. They viewed the entire Old Testament as authoritative but accepted oral tradition as equally authoritative. To them, studying the Law was a form of worship. They believed in life after death, the resurrection, and the existence of angels and spirits. They believed the way to God was through obeying the Law. Their goals were to achieve and maintain their own religious position and power.

The Herodians were a political party aligned with King Herod. Their goal was to maintain Herod's position and power. Some people think they were Sadducees, but the most important aspect of their activity was political. Herod was a puppet of Rome, which installed him as king of the Jews, so anyone who opposed Herod opposed Caesar.*

Does this commentary help you understand the Pharisees and Herodians' questions and Jesus' answers?

DAY FIVE

The Sadducees were a smaller religious sect than the Pharisees, consisting mostly of upper-class Jews. They were often descended from priests and wealthier than the Pharisees, who were mostly middle-class merchants and tradesmen. The Sadducees accepted only the first five books of the Old Testament (the Torah) as authoritative and were rigid in observing the Law. However, they rejected divine providence, resurrection (as Mark points out in verse 18), life after death (including judgment), and the existence of angels, demons, and spirits. They opposed oral law as obligatory or binding. †

Read Mark 12:18-27. What's the question, who asked it, and what was Jesus' answer? Note that Jesus said people were "mistaken"[5] in verse 24 and "greatly mistaken" in verse 27. What were the two issues? What were they "mistaken" about? What were they "greatly mistaken" about?

---

* Adapted from "Major Events in Israel's History," *The New Inductive Study Bible* (Eugene, OR: Harvest House, 2000), 2092-93.

† Adapted from "Major Events in Israel's History," *The New Inductive Study Bible* (Eugene, OR: Harvest House, 2000), 2092-93.

DAY SIX

Read Mark 12:28-44. Who questions Jesus next, and what is the question? How is this event different from the previous two? What is the theological issue, and what does Jesus say about the inquirer based on his reply?

What question does Jesus ask and answer in verses 35-37? What is the main point?

What is the main point of verses 38-40? Compare this with Matthew 6:1-6,16.

And what's the main point of verses 41-44? How does it relate to the point in verses 38-40?

Finally, record a theme for Mark 12 on MARK AT A GLANCE.

DAY SEVEN

 Store in your heart: Mark 12:29-31
Read and discuss: Mark 12

QUESTIONS FOR DISCUSSION OR INDIVIDUAL STUDY

- ∾ Discuss your insights about the parable of the vineyard.

- ∾ What principle does Jesus teach in His answer to the Pharisees and Herodians' question?

- ∾ What do you learn from the question-and-answer exchange between the Sadducees and Jesus?

- ∾ Discuss your insights from the exchange between the scribe and Jesus.

- ❧ Why is the Christ (Messiah) called the Son of David?

- ❧ What character trait was Jesus warning the people to beware of in verses 38-40? What principle does this teach?

- ❧ Discuss what you learned about giving.

- ❧ What applications to your life can you make this week from this chapter?

THOUGHT FOR THE WEEK

Before Jesus began His ministry, He spent 40 days in the Judean wilderness being tempted by Satan. Matthew records a dialogue between Jesus and Satan that Mark doesn't. Satan offered Jesus opportunities to test God, provide for Himself, and worship Satan. Jesus passed all three tests with flying colors. To each one Jesus responded with Scripture—we should not tempt God; man does not live by bread alone, but by every word that proceeds out of the mouth of God; and we should worship God alone.

The Greek word translated *tempt* in this scenario is the same one translated *test* in Mark 12. Satan tempted Jesus to sin so He would be disqualified from sinlessly atoning for man's sin. The Pharisees and other Jewish leaders tried to trap Jesus so they could accuse Him, arrest Him, and end His ministry. The Scripture doesn't indicate that these religious leaders understood Jesus' ultimate task of sacrifice. They saw Him merely as a rival, a leader who diminished their influence over the people, and so they wanted to get rid of Him.

So the motives of Satan and these religious leaders were essentially the same. They wanted to get rid of Jesus. Neither wanted to lose a grip on the people. Ultimately these religious leaders were agents of Satan. They had the same goal—to prevent God's plan.

Jesus, of course, is not just man; He's also God. So He knew what they were doing and answered their attacks. We're not God, but we do have God as our resident Teacher. God the Holy Spirit indwells each of us for a specific mission: to help us.

In John's Gospel, Jesus calls the Holy Spirit the Helper. Jesus taught that the Holy Spirit will teach us all things and bring to our remembrance everything He taught His disciples. So we know that when we need help under fire, we have a Helper, and that Helper is God Himself. We don't have to go through testing alone and on our own power. God Himself is with us in every test.

That's why James wrote in his letter that we should count trials as joy (James 1:2). Trials produce endurance and maturity. When we persevere under trial and are approved (we pass the test and are shown to be genuine), we will receive the crown of life Jesus promised to all who love Him (James 1:12).

If our perseverance is motivated by love for Christ, it proves we really are His disciples. Passing this test means we receive the reward due all who are really His—the crown of life. We don't earn eternal life by persevering; rather, because we have eternal life, because we have believed and have the Helper, the Holy Spirit, we persevere. Our perseverance is an outcome of salvation, not the cause of salvation. It's proof of salvation.

So when people put you to the test, when they challenge you about your faith, call on the Helper. Stand firm in your faith, trusting in God Himself to give you the right words to answer. After all, they're His words.

WHEN JESUS COMES BACK

Years ago a teenager asked me, "What if Jesus has already come and we don't know it?" The idea was that Jesus could be here in disguise. After all, the Jews didn't recognize Him as the Messiah when He came the first time; He looked like any other Jewish man. Why should it be any different when He comes back? Well, will it be different?

DAY ONE

Read Mark 13 today, marking key words and phrases from your bookmark. Mark *war* and *famine* but don't add them to your bookmark. Don't forget references to time; they're very important in this chapter.

DAY TWO

Make lists today from the key words you've marked. List the order of events in this chapter and note the way the events relate to what Jesus taught His disciples about what is to happen to Him.

DAY THREE

Read verses 1-13. What prompted Jesus' description of the events leading up to His return?

Herod was called "the Great" because of his magnificent building programs. Among other projects, he renovated the temple the Jews built more than 500 years earlier after they returned from exile. That second temple wasn't as beautiful as Solomon's, which the Babylonians destroyed. (Read Haggai 2:3.) But Herod's renovation had lasted at least 46 years by the time Jesus visited it, and it lasted at least another 30 years after that even though Herod died only 15 years into the project.

What did the disciples ask Jesus?

What was Jesus' first concern in His answer? What will happen that might mislead His disciples?

List what will happen before "the end." What relevance do these things have to today's events?

What principles in this chapter can you apply to your life?

DAY FOUR

Read verses 14-23. List what happens when "the abomination of desolation" stands where it shouldn't.

Matthew says Daniel spoke about the abomination of desolation. Let's do a little cross-referencing to see if we can determine what this means. Read Matthew 24:15 and Daniel 9:24-27. You can use our study on Daniel to learn more about this passage, but for now look at verse 27. What words in this verse are also in Mark 13:14?

What words in Daniel 9:26 relate this passage to Mark 13?

Remember the topic that started this chapter. In Daniel 9, what do the words *holy place* and *sanctuary* refer to?

Look at Mark 13:14. Why should people in Judea flee? How bad will this "tribulation" (verses 19 and 24) be?

DAY FIVE

Read these passages:

Isaiah 13:6-13

Joel 2:2-11

Joel 2:31-32

Joel 3:14-15

Mark 13:24

Look for words that match. What event is described in the cross-references? When will this event occur according to Mark 13:24?

What do you learn about Jesus in Mark 13:26-27?

DAY SIX

Read Mark 13:28-37. How does Jesus' parable relate to everything you've studied so far in Mark 13?

When will the things described in Mark 13 happen according to verse 32?

Why do we need to know these truths? What are we supposed to do? What key repeated command occurs in verses 33-37?

What applications from Mark 13 can and will you make to your own life?

We can't fully explore the phrase *the day of the Lord* in this survey course because the topic cuts across many books of the Bible. And when you study other texts, you'll find other related events. Just for a teaser, read 1 Thessalonians 4:13–5:10.

Now you're going to have to study 1 Thessalonians, Joel, Daniel, Revelation, and others because you have become curious, haven't you? Take your time, and don't leap to conclusions!

Finally, record a theme for Mark 13 on MARK AT A GLANCE.

DAY SEVEN

 Store in your heart: Mark 13:11

Read and discuss: Mark 13; Daniel 9:24-27; Matthew 24:15

QUESTIONS FOR DISCUSSION OR INDIVIDUAL STUDY

- ∾ Start by reviewing the sequence of events in Mark 13:1-27. Weave in the cross-references. See if you can come to a consensus about the sequencing.

- ∾ How does the phrase "the day of the Lord" (1 Thessalonians 5:2) relate to the tribulation "in those days" (Matthew 13:24)?

- ∾ How did the parable at the end of the chapter help you understand Jesus' teaching?

- ∾ What applications from Mark 13 can you make to your life? How can you use what you've learned to help others?

THOUGHT FOR THE WEEK

What will Jesus' return be like? What will He look like? How will we know when it happens? Will we see signs beforehand that signal His coming? Many people speculate about these things, but the good news is that God's Word is clear. There's no "what if" about it. He told us in advance.

One day, the disciples remarked to Jesus about how beautiful the temple Herod the Great had remodeled, refurbished, and expanded was. Jesus' reply must have stunned them. He said the temple will be torn down. That piqued their curiosity! They wanted to know when it would happen and what the signs would be.

Jesus' response to those two questions must have been equally stunning. It wasn't just about the temple being destroyed, but about persecution, war, betrayal, and even death. It was about a desecration of the temple and a great tribulation like nothing since the creation of the world. He predicted that people will claim that the Messiah is already here or there. False prophets and Christs will arise!

But the real Messiah's return will be obvious. He'll return in clouds with great power and glory and will send angels to gather the believing remnant from all over the earth. No one will have any doubt about who the real Messiah is when He comes. No one will miss this event, but only those who believe God's Word will "see" (understand) the signs. Only they will be prepared, because they believe.

Unbelievers will be surprised—the day of the Lord will come on them like a thief in the night. They will interpret the signs simply as the worst natural disasters they have ever seen. They will curse God for causing them, and they will reject the fact that they cause them by their own unbelief and immorality. They will think God is unfair because no one deserves to be punished by death. And that's because they reject God's truth that the wages of sin is death. They refuse to believe in holiness and righteousness and that they've been given chance after chance to believe. As Peter says, they are "willingly ignorant" (2 Peter 3:5 KJV). They reject knowledge (Hosea 4:6).

That day is coming, but right now, it's not too late. The gospel must be preached to all the nations first. We still have time to rescue more people. At the end of the movie *Schindler's List*, Oskar Schindler laments that he could have rescued one more if he had sold his gold pin or ring. One more, one more! He knew the awful reality of Jews dying in the Holocaust. He saw it!

Do we understand the awful reality of the second death, the lake of fire? What will we do to save one more? One more? Do we believe the description Jesus gives of the tribulation in those days? What will we give up to help one more not go through that? Will we give up our prized possessions? Will we see one life as more valuable than the precious things we own? Do we think we have lots of time? Do we think we can wait? One more!

THE SPIRIT IS WILLING, BUT THE FLESH IS WEAK

Intentions can be good, and boasting is easy. The follow-through, however, is much more difficult. We make promises we don't always keep. We look at other people and so easily notice their faults and shortcomings. But we should remove the logs from our own eyes before we try to take the specks out of others'.

DAY ONE

Read Mark 14 and observe the order of events. Again, time phrases are important. You might want to write the events in the margins of your Bible before marking anything other than the time phrases. Then reread Mark 14 and mark the key words and phrases from your bookmark.

DAY TWO

Today read the chapter again event by event and see if you find any more key words or people you want to mark in particular parts of the story. They don't have to be key in more than one paragraph or story. The idea is to focus on the details to uncover insights. Often when a story is familiar, we'll skim through it and miss important details. So slow down and enjoy your reading today. If you want to make lists or record sequences or insights, go ahead.

DAY THREE

Understanding the Jewish feast of Passover is important if you want to understand the New Testament. (See, for example, 1 Corinthians 5:7-8.) The first Passover occurred in Egypt just before the Exodus. Read Exodus 12:1-27; 13:1-16 and Deuteronomy 16:1-16 to familiarize yourself with the Passover (Unleavened Bread).

Jesus and His family obeyed Deuteronomy 16:16, as Luke 2:41 records. Today, observant Jews and even nonreligious Jews celebrate the Passover. Not all travel to Jerusalem to observe the feast, but family gatherings begin with a meal at which the story is recounted. Without the temple, unblemished lambs are not sacrificed, and today lamb isn't even eaten. But the tradition is replayed with various foods, readings, and songs.

In Jesus' day, the Roman *triclinium*, a U-shaped low table, was common, and diners reclined on pillows on the floor, leaning on one elbow with feet away from the table. Food was eaten family style with bowls spaced around the table so all could reach without passing dishes. Bread and wine were also part of the meal.

DAY FOUR

Read Mark 14:32-40 today. Then read Mark 11:19, Luke 21:37, and John 18:1-2. *Garden* can mean "grove of trees," and *Gethsemane* is a translation of Hebrew terms for "olive press." A grove of olive trees at the base of the Mount of Olives, just across the Kidron Valley from the Temple Mount, is known today as the Garden of Gethsemane.

Now let's ask some of the 5 W's and an H about this passage. What did Jesus do on this particular night? Who went with Him? What did He ask them to do, and what did they do? Have you ever been like these disciples? What message can we learn from this event today?

DAY FIVE

Today let's look at Mark 14:41-52. What do we know about Judas's betrayal? Read the following, asking the 5 W's and an H as you go:

> Mark 14:10-11
>
> Luke 22:1-7
>
> John 6:70-71
>
> John 12:1-8
>
> Acts 2:22-23

The names of a few people in the Bible are generally identified with the quality of their characters. One is Judas. The world knows what a "Judas" is—someone who betrays another. But the real force behind Judas was Satan, who couldn't defeat Jesus in the temptation in the wilderness and who now thinks victory is near.

DAY SIX

For our last day of study this week, let's look at verses 53-72. Underline, highlight, or mark *testimony* and *witness*[6] if you haven't already done so. In this mock trial, was the Sanhedrin able to convict Jesus? What does this tell you about the religious authorities? How did they decide to prosecute Him?

Now let's shift our focus to Peter. If you haven't marked *Peter*, go ahead and mark his name but not the pronouns. Read Mark 14:27-31,37-38 and then review Mark 14:54,66-72. What do you think about Peter? How do you think you would have acted if you were in his situation? Have you ever acted the way Peter did in this event?

Finally, record a theme for Mark 14 on MARK AT A GLANCE.

DAY SEVEN

Store in your heart: Mark 14:38
Read and discuss: Mark 14

QUESTIONS FOR DISCUSSION OR INDIVIDUAL STUDY

- Review the sequence of events in Mark 14 before digging into any specific part of it.

- Discuss the significance of the Passover. What elements have carried over into our worship?

- ∿ Discuss Judas's betrayal and its relationship to prophecy.

- ∿ What did you learn about Jesus' mock trial before the Sanhedrin (council)?

- ∿ What did you learn about yourself from Peter's example?

- ∿ What lessons about prayer does this chapter contain?

THOUGHT FOR THE WEEK

Peter was one of three disciples closest to Jesus. He was with James and John when Jesus raised the daughter of a synagogue official from the dead. The same three were with Jesus on the Mount of Transfiguration and again in the Garden of Gethsemane just before His arrest.

Peter was the first disciple Jesus called and clearly the most impetuous. When the disciples saw Jesus walking on the Sea of Galilee, Peter got out of the boat and walked on the water to meet Him. He confessed Jesus as the Christ, the Son of the Living God, and later cut off the high priest's slave's ear when Jesus was arrested.

Peter made bold assertions, like promising the Lord he would die with Him rather than fall away. Granted, the others said the same, but Peter was first. Jesus replied that Peter would deny Him three times that very night, before a rooster crowed twice. And he did.

After Peter made this showy promise to endure, Jesus took Peter, James, and John away from the others in the Garden, and then Jesus went on alone to pray. Before doing so, He asked them to do one thing: watch for an hour. But they slept.

This happened two more times.

At the high priest's house, false witnesses made up

accusations against Jesus. The Sanhedrin had no credible evidence to condemn Jesus to death, but Jesus condemned Himself by confessing the truth. Peter, warming himself by a fire in the courtyard while Jesus was spat on, beaten, and slapped, denied that he was one of Jesus' companions. If he confessed, he too might have been killed.

The rooster crowed. Three times Peter denied Jesus, just as he had fallen asleep three times.

How easily we can sit in our comfortable circumstances and criticize Peter. How easily we can say, "Not me. I wouldn't do that!" But haven't we already done that? Do we faithfully keep watching and praying so we don't come into temptation? Or do we deny Jesus when we are under fire from His opponents?

We may think we have strong faith, but how much has our faith been tested? When really hard times come, how do we measure up? Are we willing to stand up and say, "Yes, I'm one of His followers"? When faced with a choice, do we choose the easy way?

Our brothers and sisters around the world have opportunities to take the easy way, the way of denial. They could renounce their faith to save their lives, but many of them don't. They go to prison. Some are killed.

In the West, we don't face those circumstances. Christianity has so dominated the culture that Christians aren't thrown in prison or enslaved or murdered for their faith. But in many places Christianity is a threat to established majority religions. Lives are at stake. And yet believers stand firm.

So watch and pray that you don't enter into temptation— the temptation to deny your faith in a situation like Peter's. "The spirit is willing, but the flesh is weak" (Matthew 26:41). We have the Holy Spirit to strengthen us, but our flesh gives in to temptation.

Watch and pray!

DESPAIR

Corrie ten Boom once said, "When you enter a tunnel on a train, you don't throw away your ticket and jump off, you sit still and trust the engineer." Jesus was tried, convicted, and executed. The trial was a farce, the no-appeal sentence was unjust, and the punishment was cruel. Jesus was dead and buried. Would His disciples despair, or would they have hope?

DAY ONE

Read Mark 15, marking key words and phrases from your bookmark as usual. Remember to keep track of time references. You also may find it helpful to mark important names in this chapter, such as *Pilate*.

DAY TWO

Mark in the margin of your Bible or list in your notebook the sequence of events. Pilate, the Roman governor of the Roman province of Judea, made his headquarters at the Praetorium, which was located at the Antonia Fortress.

See the map in the appendix called "Jerusalem of the New Testament."

Read Matthew 27:19-25 and Luke 23:13-23. (In Luke 23:6-12, Luke recounts that Pilate sent Jesus to Herod, and Herod sent Him back.) What did you learn about Pilate? What did he know? How did he act?

DAY THREE

Several details of Jesus' scourging and crucifixion were fulfillments of Old Testament prophecy. Read the following passages and compare them to Mark 15: Isaiah 52:13–53:12; Psalm 22:1-18.

Many believe that quoting the first line of a psalm is equivalent to invoking more verses, even the entire psalm. In Mark 15:34, Jesus quotes the first line of Psalm 22.

DAY FOUR

Mark 15:38 says that the veil in the temple was torn in two from top to bottom. This veil separated the Holy Place from the Holy of Holies (the Most Holy Place). Before the Babylonian captivity, the Holy of Holies contained the Ark of the Covenant, which contained the Ten Commandments. Covering the ark was the mercy seat, where God met with Israel. The high priest could enter this place only once a year on the Day of Atonement, to sprinkle blood on the mercy seat to atone for the sins of Israel.

Read Hebrews 9:1–10:22. Note the mention of the veil in 10:20. Now, if it was torn from top to bottom, who tore it? What did the tearing of the physical veil in the temple represent?

John records Jesus' final words: "It is finished," which translate the one Greek verb *tetelestai*. The verb was sometimes used to indicate that a debt was paid in full (like a mortgage)—a deed was posted on a wall with *tetelestai* written across it for all to see. How does this word picture apply to the crucifixion?

Finally, record a theme for Mark 15 on MARK AT A GLANCE.

DAY FIVE

Read Mark 15:40–16:20 and note the sequence of events in your Bible or notebook. Then read Mark 16 again and mark the key words as usual.

DAY SIX

What do you think of Jesus' disciples' reaction to His death and resurrection? Do you remember what He had taught them about His death? Had He mentioned the resurrection? Review the following passages:

Mark 8:31-32

Mark 9:11-13

Mark 9:31-32

Mark 10:32-34

Mark 14:27-29

The disciples' reaction in Mark 16:11-14 seems incongruous with the command Jesus gave and even *their* actions according to verse 20. What must have occurred?

Finally, record a theme for Mark 16 on MARK AT A GLANCE.

DAY SEVEN

Store in your heart: Mark 16:6
Read and discuss: Mark 15–16

QUESTIONS FOR DISCUSSION OR INDIVIDUAL STUDY

- Discuss the sequence of events in Mark 15, including the interactions involving Pilate, the Jews, the soldiers, Joseph of Arimathea, and others.

  - What were Pilate's role and his view of Jesus?

  - How did the Jews react to Pilate's statements?

  - What interactions did Jesus have with soldiers? (Note differences before and after His death.)

  - Note the roles and actions of the other characters.

- Discuss the order of events on the first day of the week. Again, be sure to cover all the interactions involving individuals and groups, such as the women.

- How did the disciples react to the news of the resurrection? Compare their response to the good news to people's responses today.

- What did you learn from marking *believe*?

- What is the significance of the last two verses? Do they affect your life?

THOUGHT FOR THE WEEK

After Jesus ascended to heaven, He "sat down at the right hand of God" (Mark 16:19). In history, the one who sat at the right hand of any leader was second to him in power and influence. Even today we use the expression *right-hand man* for the most indispensable, trusted person. He acts for and with the authority of the person on his left. It's an exalted position, deserving respect and obedience and engendering requests for favor.

So Jesus is the Father's right-hand man and thus deserves respect and obedience. And His position gives rise to requests for favor because He can grant favor. He has the power and authority of God the Father.

One of the first actions that reflected His authority and power was sending the Holy Spirit on Pentecost. During His earthly ministry, Jesus promised another Helper of the same kind as Himself, the Holy Spirit. The Holy Spirit empowers, teaches, and causes us to remember Jesus' teachings until He returns.

An early example of this was Stephen's defense of the gospel just before the Jews stoned him to death. By the power of the Holy Spirit, he saw the glory of God in heaven and Jesus standing at the right hand of God.

Jesus sat at the right hand of God when He ascended, but interestingly, Stephen saw Him standing. Some think Jesus stood to welcome Stephen's spirit to heaven and into His presence (Steven asked the Lord to receive his spirit). Others believe Jesus stood to cheer Stephen on, to applaud his magnificent testimony to the gospel and his wonderful faith in the face of death. Another possibility is that Jesus rose to judge those who condemned Stephen. Finally, He may have stood to be Stephen's Advocate, to plead his case before the righteous Judge, God the Father.

This scene in Acts 7 in which Stephen gazes into heaven and sees Jesus at the right hand of God has another important implication. There were already witnesses to Jesus' death, burial, and resurrection. Not only the Gospels but also 1 Corinthians 15:3-8 recounts the eyewitnesses of the resurrected Jesus. Luke recounts Jesus' ascension to heaven from the Mount of Olives in his Gospel and in Acts 1. But Stephen's account is important because it provides an eyewitness to Jesus at the right hand of God. Of course Jesus prophesied this rank (Matthew 26:64; Luke 22:69), and Paul, Peter, and the author of Hebrews all speak of it, but Luke tells us Stephen *saw it*! He was an eyewitness. His accusers covered their ears and stoned him for this supposed blasphemy. But they killed Jesus for predicting He would be at the Father's right hand.

The position Jesus has at the right hand of God the Father means the Father has subjected all angels, authorities, and powers to Him. And there He sits until all His enemies are made a footstool for His feet. But there is more. In the end, Jesus will rise again from sitting beside the Father and will lead His army to earth to battle His enemies once and for all and to establish His reign on earth for 1000 years. And according to 1 Corinthians 15, when He has abolished all other rule, authority, and power and put all His enemies under His feet, He will hand over the kingdom to the Father.

The last enemy that will be conquered is death. Revelation 20 describes this last enemy's fate: At the great white throne, death will be thrown into the lake of fire. After that comes the new heaven and new earth, in which there will be no more death, crying, pain, or mourning; and a new Jerusalem in which God Almighty and the Lamb are the temple and its lamp. There, everyone will see His face. Everyone will join Stephen in witnessing the glory of God and Jesus.

Amen! Come, Lord Jesus!

Appendix

Theme of Mark:

SEGMENT DIVISIONS

		CHAPTER THEMES
		1
		2
		3
		4
		5
		6
		7
		8
		9
		10
		11
		12
		13
		14
		15
		16

Author:

Date:

Purpose:

Key Words:

immediately

authority (power)

kingdom of God

mark every reference to Satan or demons

covenant

Spirit

REGIONS FROM WHICH
PEOPLE CAME TO SEE JESUS

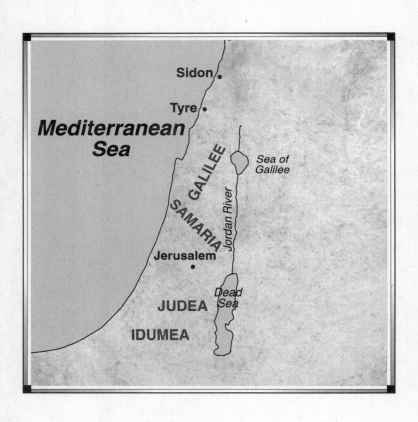

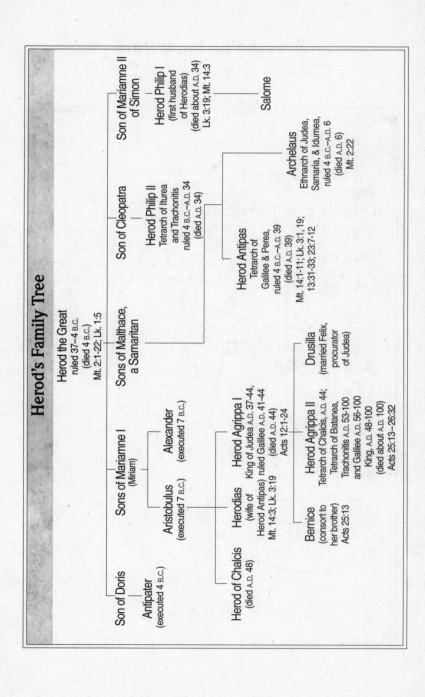

Herod's Family Tree

Herod the Great
ruled 37–4 B.C.
(died 4 B.C.)
Mt. 2:1-22; Lk. 1:5

Son of Doris

Antipater
(executed 4 B.C.)

Sons of Mariamne I (Miriam)

Aristobulus
(executed 7 B.C.)

Alexander
(executed 7 B.C.)

Herod of Chalcis
(died A.D. 48)

Herodias
(wife of
Herod Antipas)
Mt. 14:3; Lk. 3:19

Herod Agrippa I
King of Judea A.D. 37-44,
ruled Galilee A.D. 41-44
(died A.D. 44)
Acts 12:1-24

Bernice
(consort to
her brother)
Acts 25:13

Herod Agrippa II
Tetrarch of Chalcis, A.D. 44;
Tetrarch of Batanea,
Trachonitis A.D. 53-100
and Galilee A.D. 56-100
King, A.D. 48-100
(died about A.D. 100)
Acts 25:13 – 26:32

Drusilla
(married Felix,
procurator
of Judea)

Sons of Malthace, a Samaritan

Herod Antipas
Tetrarch of
Galilee & Perea,
ruled 4 B.C.–A.D. 39
(died A.D. 39)
Mt. 14:1-11; Lk. 3:1, 19;
13:31-33; 23:7-12

Archelaus
Ethnarch of Judea,
Samaria, & Idumea,
ruled 4 B.C.–A.D. 6
(died A.D. 6)
Mt. 2:22

Son of Cleopatra

Herod Philip II
Tetrarch of Iturea
and Trachonitis
ruled 4 B.C.–A.D. 34
(died A.D. 34)

Son of Mariamne II of Simon

Herod Philip I
(first husband
of Herodias)
(died about A.D. 34)
Lk. 3:19; Mt. 14:3

Salome

Jerusalem of the New Testament

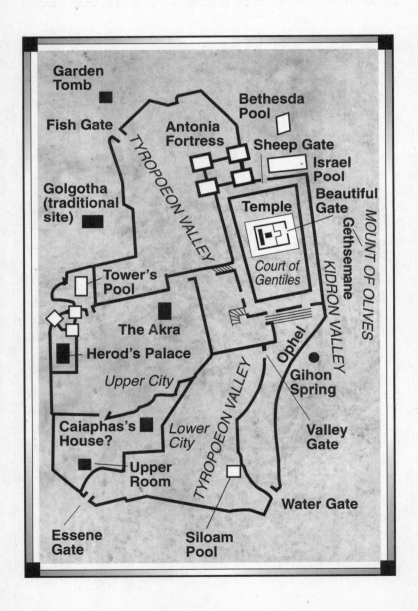

A parable is a story that is not usually literally factual but is true to life and teaches a universal moral lesson or truth. The details of a parable reinforce the main theme, so you don't have to ascribe primary spiritual meaning and application to each point.

Jesus frequently used parables in His teaching for two reasons: to reveal truth to believers and hide it from those who rejected it because their hearts were hardened.

Here are some steps that can help you interpret a parable properly:

1. *Determine the occasion of the parable.* A parable clarifies or emphasizes a truth, so discover why it was told. What prompted it?

2. *Look for the intended meaning of the parable.* The meaning will sometimes be stated. If not, it usually can be determined by its application to the audience.

3. *Don't impose any meaning beyond what the speaker clearly stated or applied to the hearers.*

4. *Identify the central idea of the parable.* Every parable has a central theme or emphasis. Don't ascribe meaning to details of the story if they're independent of the main teaching of the parable. Since a parable has one central point or emphasis, identify relevant details. Again, a detail is relevant only if it reinforces the central theme of the parable.

Surely you have heard sermons on the parable of the prodigal son. Many teachers miss the occasion and meaning of this parable, including the original meaning of the word *prodigal*, which, by the way, does not appear in the Scripture. (A prodigal was originally one who wastefully spent his inheritance. Only after this parable's popularity did it also refer to someone who returned after an absence.)

People attach all sorts of meanings to the details of the story. But Jesus told this parable because He wanted the Pharisees to see what their hearts were like as they grumbled, "This man receives sinners and eats with them" (Luke 15:2). In order to make His point, Jesus told three consecutive parables about three things that were lost: a sheep, a coin, and a son. In each of the parables Jesus uses the following words: *lost, found, sin,* and *joy (rejoice).* When He gets to the story of the prodigal son, He contrasts the kindness of the father's heart with the hardness of the elder brother's, and in so doing, He shows the Pharisees that their hearts are like the elder brother's.

5. *Interpret parables in the context of first-century culture, not today's culture.* For example, in the parable of the wise and foolish virgins, the central emphasis of the parable is this: "Be on the alert then, for you do not know the day nor the hour" (Matthew 25:13). Understanding Eastern wedding traditions gives insight into the parable and explains why some were ready and others were not.

6. *Do not establish doctrine when parables are the primary or only source for that teaching.* Parables generally amplify or affirm doctrine rather than establishing it.

Notes

1. NIV: good news
2. KJV: straightway, forthwith; NKJV: at once; NIV: without delay, quickly, as soon as, at once; ESV: at once
3. NIV: teachers of the law
4. NIV, ESV: [this phrase does not appear because the verse isn't found in early manuscripts]
5. KJV: err; NIV: in error; ESV: wrong
6. NIV: evidence (once)

Books in the
New Inductive Study Series

❧ ❧ ❧ ❧

Teach Me Your Ways
GENESIS, EXODUS,
LEVITICUS, NUMBERS, DEUTERONOMY

Choosing Victory,
Overcoming Defeat
JOSHUA, JUDGES, RUTH

Desiring God's Own Heart
1 & 2 SAMUEL, 1 CHRONICLES

Walking Faithfully with God
1 & 2 KINGS, 2 CHRONICLES

Overcoming Fear
and Discouragement
EZRA, NEHEMIAH, ESTHER

Trusting God
in Times of Adversity
JOB

Praising God Through
Prayer and Worship
PSALMS

God's Answers for
Today's Problems
PROVERBS

Walking with God
in Every Season
ECCLESIASTES, SONG OF SOLOMON,
LAMENTATIONS

Face-to-Face with a Holy God
ISAIAH

God's Blueprint
for Bible Prophecy
DANIEL

Discovering the God
of Second Chances
JONAH, JOEL, AMOS, OBADIAH

Finding Hope
When Life Seems Dark
HOSEA, MICAH, NAHUM,
HABAKKUK, ZEPHANIAH

Opening the Windows
of Blessing
HAGGAI, ZECHARIAH, MALACHI

The Coming of God's Kingdom
MATTHEW

Experiencing the Miracles of Jesus
MARK

The Call to Follow Jesus
LUKE

The God Who Cares
and Knows You
JOHN

The Holy Spirit
Unleashed in You
ACTS

God's Answers for
Relationships and Passions
1 & 2 CORINTHIANS

Free from Bondage
God's Way
GALATIANS, EPHESIANS

That I May Know Him
PHILIPPIANS, COLOSSIANS

Standing Firm in
These Last Days
1 & 2 THESSALONIANS

Walking in Power,
Love, and Discipline
1 & 2 TIMOTHY, TITUS

The Key to Living by Faith
HEBREWS

Living with Discernment
in the End Times
1 & 2 PETER, JUDE

God's Love Alive in You
1, 2, & 3 JOHN,
PHILEMON, JAMES

Behold, Jesus Is Coming!
REVELATION